Contents

How to use this book

Each page has a title telling you what it is about.

Instructions look like this. Always read these carefully before starting.

Read these word problems very carefully. Decide how you will work out the answers.

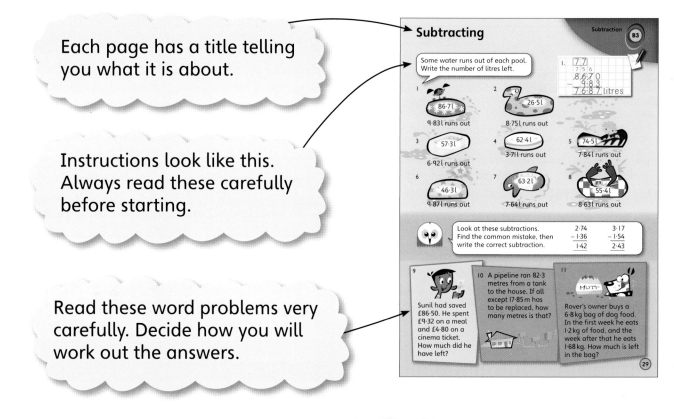

This shows you how to set out your work. The first question is done for you.

This is Owl. Ask your teacher if you need to do his questions.

These are exploratory activities. You may want to discuss them with a partner.

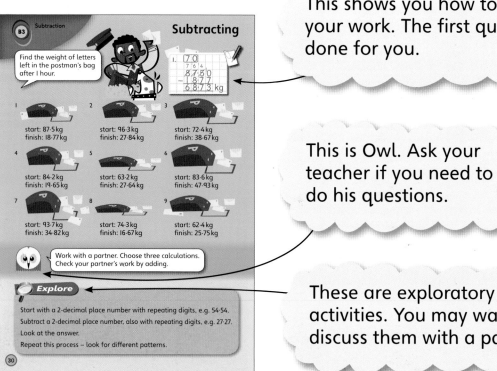

Negative numbers

1 Write the position of each letter.

1. a) ⁻1

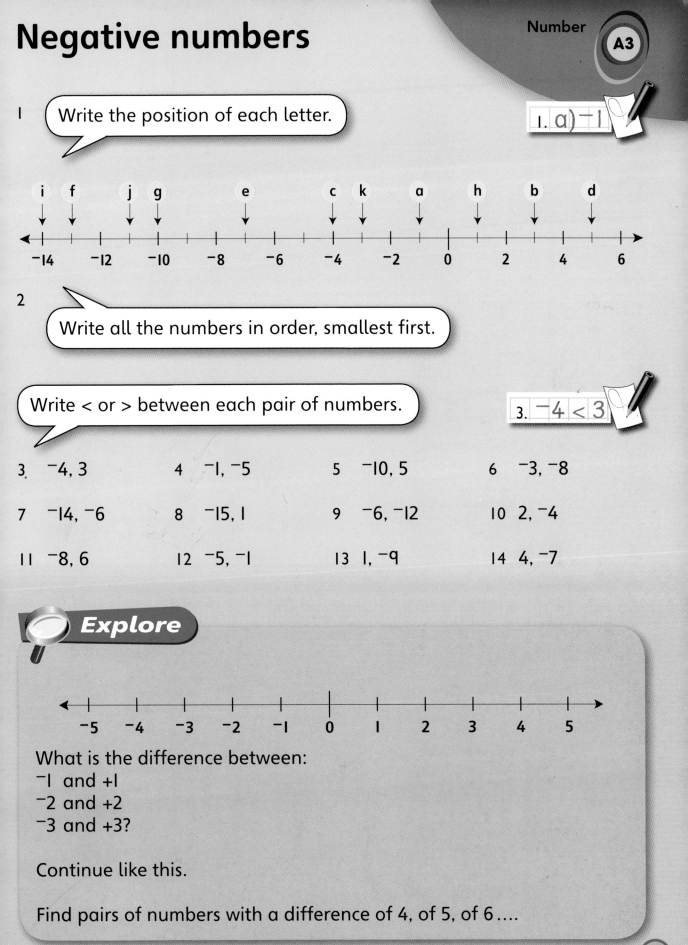

2 Write all the numbers in order, smallest first.

Write < or > between each pair of numbers.

3. ⁻4 < 3

3 ⁻4, 3   4 ⁻1, ⁻5   5 ⁻10, 5   6 ⁻3, ⁻8

7 ⁻14, ⁻6   8 ⁻15, 1   9 ⁻6, ⁻12   10 2, ⁻4

11 ⁻8, 6   12 ⁻5, ⁻1   13 1, ⁻9   14 4, ⁻7

Explore

What is the difference between:
⁻1 and +1
⁻2 and +2
⁻3 and +3?

Continue like this.

Find pairs of numbers with a difference of 4, of 5, of 6 ....

3

Negative numbers

1 Write the position of each letter.

1. a) $^-3$

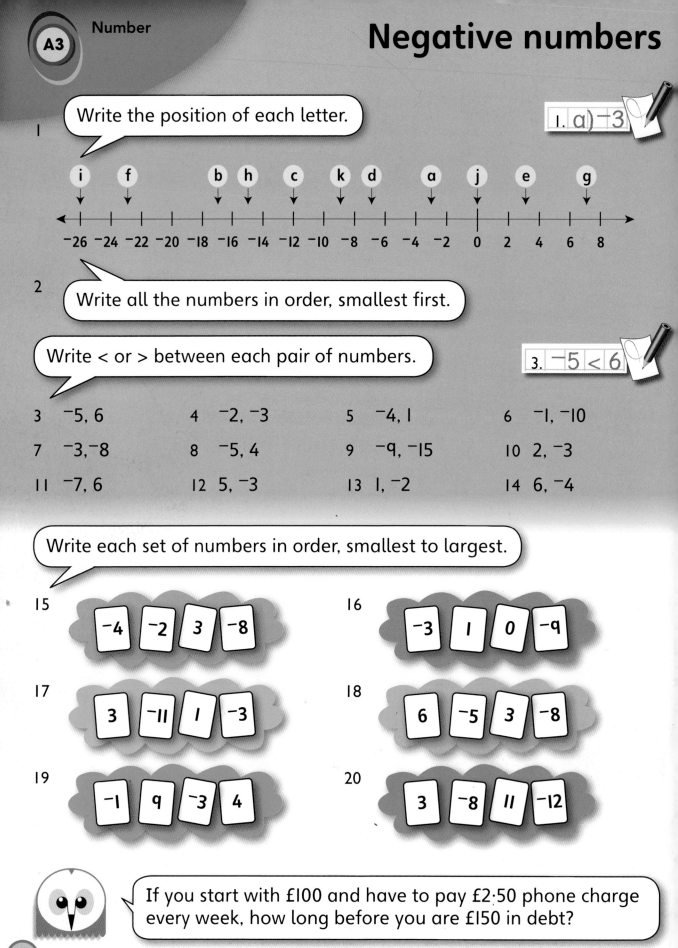

2 Write all the numbers in order, smallest first.

Write < or > between each pair of numbers.

3. $^-5 < 6$

3	$^-5$, 6	4	$^-2$, $^-3$	5	$^-4$, 1	6	$^-1$, $^-10$
7	$^-3$, $^-8$	8	$^-5$, 4	9	$^-9$, $^-15$	10	2, $^-3$
11	$^-7$, 6	12	5, $^-3$	13	1, $^-2$	14	6, $^-4$

Write each set of numbers in order, smallest to largest.

15 $^-4$ $^-2$ 3 $^-8$

16 $^-3$ 1 0 $^-9$

17 3 $^-11$ 1 $^-3$

18 6 $^-5$ 3 $^-8$

19 $^-1$ 9 $^-3$ 4

20 3 $^-8$ 11 $^-12$

If you start with £100 and have to pay £2·50 phone charge every week, how long before you are £150 in debt?

Negative numbers

Use the thermometer to help you write each set of temperatures in order, lowest first.

1. ⁻10°, ⁻1°, 4°

1 4°, ⁻1°, ⁻10°   2 ⁻2°, 0°, ⁻6°

3 ⁻10°, ⁻9°, ⁻15°   4 ⁻7°, 9°, ⁻8°, 6°

5 5°, ⁻7°, ⁻1°, 9°, ⁻6°   6 ⁻7°, 4°, 12°

7 ⁻8°, 4°, ⁻6°, 14°   8 ⁻2°, 9°, 1°, 0°, ⁻8°

9 5°, ⁻3°, ⁻7°, ⁻9°   10 12°, ⁻15°, 10°, ⁻8°, ⁻4°

11 6°, ⁻7°, 12°, ⁻9°   12 5°, ⁻1°, ⁻6°, ⁻8°, 3°

Write the temperature:

13. ⁻1°

13   3° warmer than Paris
14   2° warmer than Moscow
15   4° colder than London
16   5° warmer than New York
17   10° warmer than Antarctica
18   10° colder than Warsaw
19   8° warmer than New York
20   15° warmer than Antarctica
21   4° colder than Moscow
22   4° colder than Paris

Place	Temperature in °C
London	⁻2°
Paris	⁻4°
Warsaw	⁻8°
Moscow	⁻16°
New York	⁻5°
Antarctica	⁻20°

Write three places you know and their approximate temperatures in January.

5

Negative numbers

Complete the missing temperatures.

1. up 3° = ⁻2°, ...

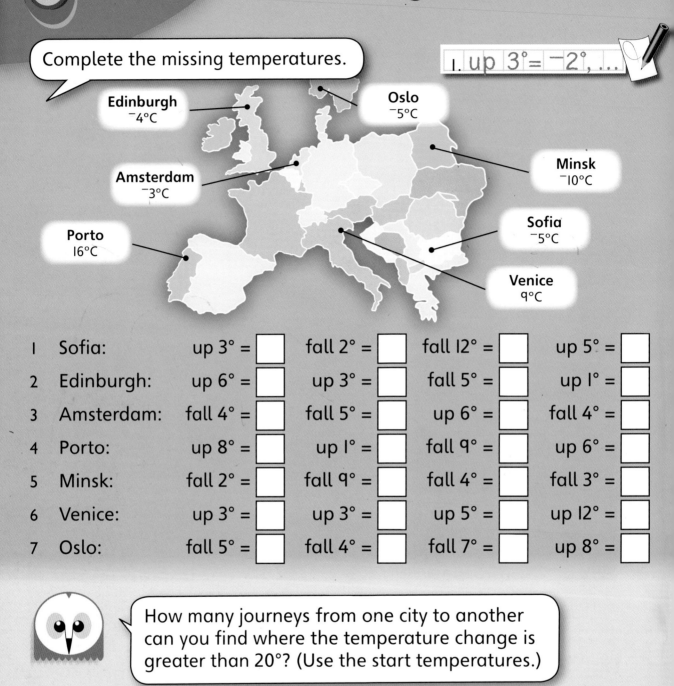

Edinburgh ⁻4°C

Oslo ⁻5°C

Minsk ⁻10°C

Amsterdam ⁻3°C

Porto 16°C

Sofia ⁻5°C

Venice 9°C

		up 3° =	fall 2° =	fall 12° =	up 5° =
1	Sofia:	up 3° =	fall 2° =	fall 12° =	up 5° =
2	Edinburgh:	up 6° =	up 3° =	fall 5° =	up 1° =
3	Amsterdam:	fall 4° =	fall 5° =	up 6° =	fall 4° =
4	Porto:	up 8° =	up 1° =	fall 9° =	up 6° =
5	Minsk:	fall 2° =	fall 9° =	fall 4° =	fall 3° =
6	Venice:	up 3° =	up 3° =	up 5° =	up 12° =
7	Oslo:	fall 5° =	fall 4° =	fall 7° =	up 8° =

How many journeys from one city to another can you find where the temperature change is greater than 20°? (Use the start temperatures.)

Each monster owes £10. Write their debt.

8. ⁻£7

8 has £3

9 has £5

10 has £1

11 has ⁻£12

Percentages

Write 10% of each amount.

1. 10% of £14 = £1·40

1 £14

2 £11

3 £12

4 £5

5 £13

6 £8

7 £9

8 £15

Now write 20% of each price.

Write 10% of each length in centimetres.

9. 10% of 14 = 1·4 m
1·4 m = 140 cm

9 14 m

10 7 m

11 6 m

12 4 m

13 750 cm

14 8 m

15 3400 cm

16 22 m

17 18 m

18 230 cm

19 54 m

20 1200 cm

Is your class more or less than 10% of the school? What about other classes?

Percentages

Find the matching pairs of fractions and percentages.

1. $\frac{1}{2} = 50\%$

1

$\frac{1}{4}$ 10% $\frac{1}{5}$ 75% $\frac{1}{100}$ 50% $\frac{1}{8}$

1% $\frac{1}{2}$ 20% $\frac{3}{4}$ 25% $\frac{1}{10}$ 12·5%

Find 10% of the amount. Use this to find the percentage given.

2. $10\% \text{ of } £12 = £1·20$
$30\% = £3·60$

2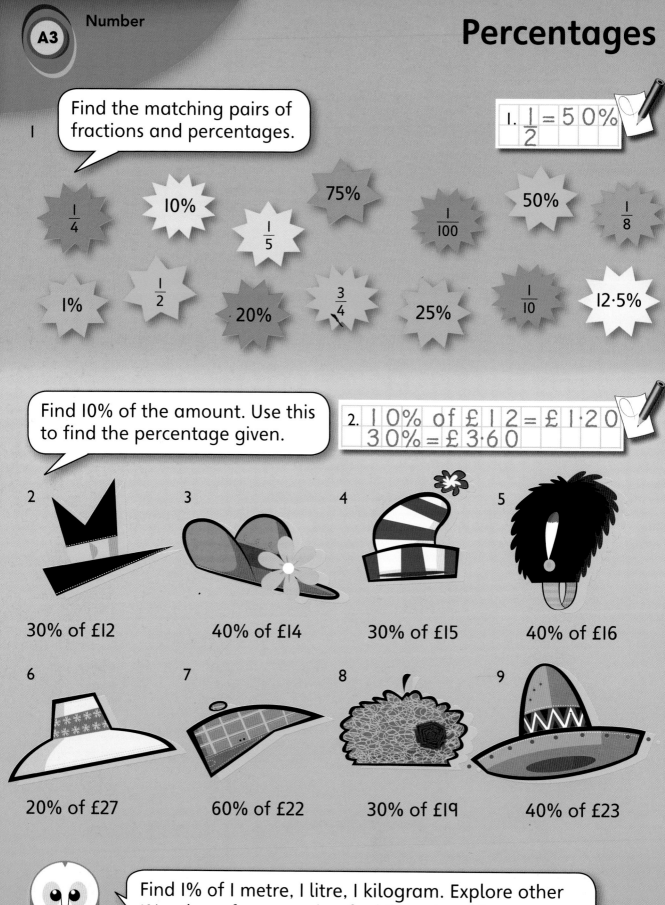
30% of £12

3
40% of £14

4
30% of £15

5
40% of £16

6
20% of £27

7
60% of £22

8
30% of £19

9
40% of £23

Find 1% of 1 metre, 1 litre, 1 kilogram. Explore other 1% values, for example of a kilometre, of a tonne....

Percentages

1 Copy and complete the table.

Fraction	$\frac{1}{2}$		$\frac{1}{10}$	$\frac{1}{5}$	$\frac{2}{5}$	$\frac{3}{10}$			$\frac{4}{5}$		$\frac{3}{4}$	$\frac{1}{8}$
Percentage	50%	25%					70%	1%		60%		

Find the VAT for each item.

2. 10% of £12 = £1·20
5% of £12 = £0·60
2·5% of £12 = £0·30
17·5% of £12 = £2·10

2 Karaoke £12

3 BLING £18

4 Hip Hop £16 Years

5 ROCK £14

6 POP £22

7 Chill £26

If VAT was raised to 20%, how much more would each item cost?

Copy and complete.

8. 10% = 180
30% = 540
1% = 18
31% = 558

8 31% of 1800

9 21% of 1400

10 26% of 1200

11 52% of 800

12 29% of 700

13 43% of 1100

14 38% of 900

15 46% of 600

Write the fraction, then write the percentage.

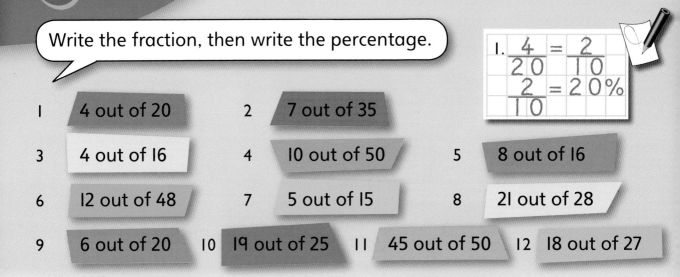

1. $\dfrac{4}{20} = \dfrac{2}{10}$
$\dfrac{2}{10} = 20\%$

1   4 out of 20

2   7 out of 35

3   4 out of 16

4   10 out of 50

5   8 out of 16

6   12 out of 48

7   5 out of 15

8   21 out of 28

9   6 out of 20

10   19 out of 25

11   45 out of 50

12   18 out of 27

Explore

Write these fractions as percentages: $\dfrac{1}{2}$, $\dfrac{1}{3}$, $\dfrac{1}{4}$, $\dfrac{1}{5}$, ...

For difficult fractions, use a calculator.

For example, for $\dfrac{1}{7}$ divide the numerator by the denominator.   0·1428571

Multiply the answer by 100.   14·28571

Round it to the nearest tenth.   14·3%

13

Sarita bought a fleece for £40. When she sold it a year later, she lost 20%. How much did she sell it for?

14

Afram saws logs. He estimates that 15% is wastage. He saws 1 tonne of logs. How many kilograms of logs are wasted?

Multiplying

Copy and complete these multiplications.

1 274×23

	200	70	4
20	4000	1400	80
3	60		

5480
+ ...

2 156×32

	100	50	6
30	3000	1500	
2			

...
+ ...

3

	300	20	6
10	3000		
8			

4

	400	30	8
20			
6			

5

	200	60	7
30			
4			

Write each as a standard multiplication.
Work them out. Are your answers the same?

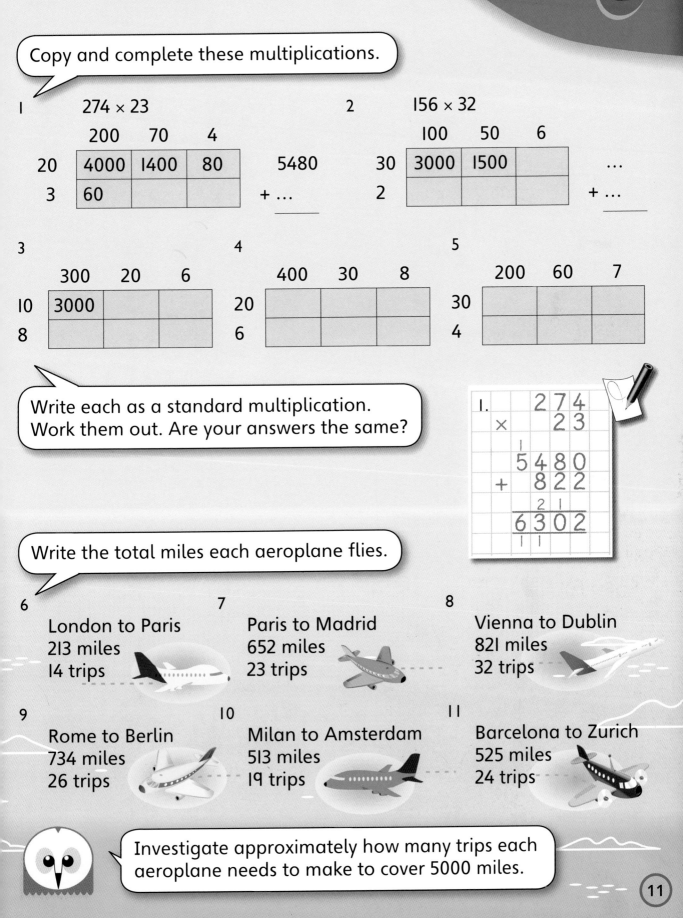

```
1.        2 7 4
     ×      2 3
          1
        5 4 8 0
     +    8 2 2
          2 1
        6 3 0 2
          1 1
```

Write the total miles each aeroplane flies.

6
London to Paris
213 miles
14 trips

7
Paris to Madrid
652 miles
23 trips

8
Vienna to Dublin
821 miles
32 trips

9
Rome to Berlin
734 miles
26 trips

10
Milan to Amsterdam
513 miles
19 trips

11
Barcelona to Zurich
525 miles
24 trips

Investigate approximately how many trips each aeroplane needs to make to cover 5000 miles.

Multiplying

Calculate the total cost of these flights.

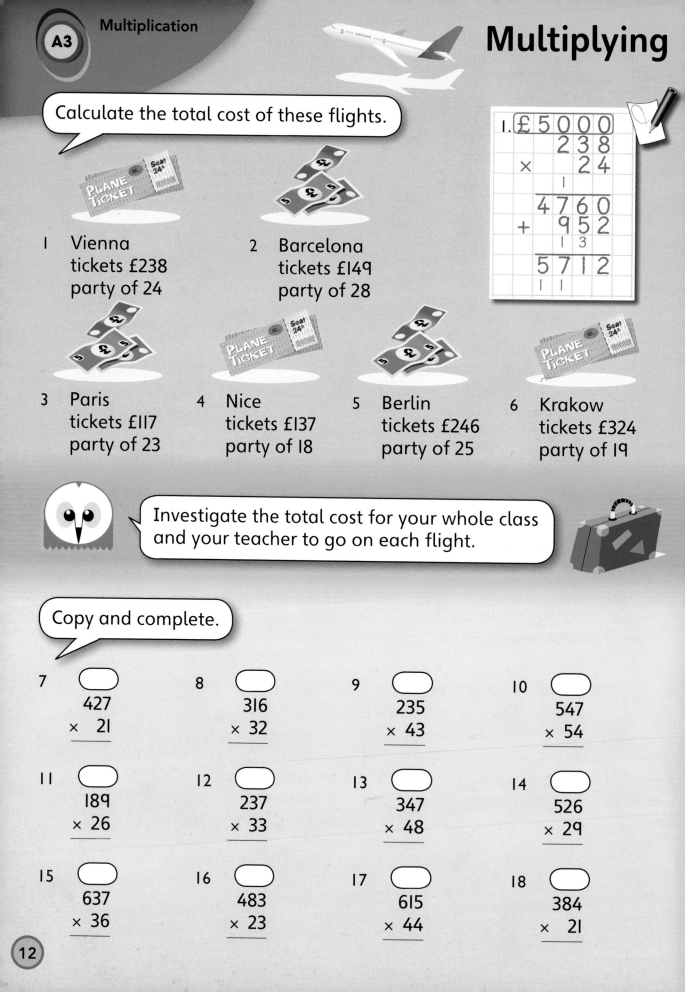

1. £5000
```
      2 3 8
  ×     2 4
        1
    4 7 6 0
  +   9 5 2
      1 3
    5 7 1 2
    1 1
```

1   Vienna
tickets £238
party of 24

2   Barcelona
tickets £149
party of 28

3   Paris
tickets £117
party of 23

4   Nice
tickets £137
party of 18

5   Berlin
tickets £246
party of 25

6   Krakow
tickets £324
party of 19

Investigate the total cost for your whole class and your teacher to go on each flight.

Copy and complete.

7
```
   427
×   21
```

8
```
   316
×   32
```

9
```
   235
×   43
```

10
```
   547
×   54
```

11
```
   189
×   26
```

12
```
   237
×   33
```

13
```
   347
×   48
```

14
```
   526
×   29
```

15
```
   637
×   36
```

16
```
   483
×   23
```

17
```
   615
×   44
```

18
```
   384
×   21
```

Multiplying

Six children took part in a multiplication challenge. Here are their answers. Who got:

1 one correct

Tim

| 473 × 26 | 524 × 18 |
| 122298 | 9462 |

Jack

| 546 × 23 | 752 × 28 |
| 12658 | 21056 |

2 both correct

Jenny

| 397 × 42 | 187 × 35 |
| 16674 | 6545 |

Su Li

| 463 × 34 | 624 × 26 |
| 15342 | 16224 |

3 none correct?

Ranjit

| 294 × 18 | 436 × 27 |
| 5392 | 1161 |

Devi

| 518 × 33 | 356 × 42 |
| 17951 | 15962 |

Write the correct answers to those that are wrong.

Investigate the number of hours in these time periods.

4 1 January to 30 April

5 1 May to 31 August

6 1 September to 31 December

7 1 March to 30 June

Work with a partner. Find the number of hours between your two birthdays.

Calculate the areas of these football pitches.

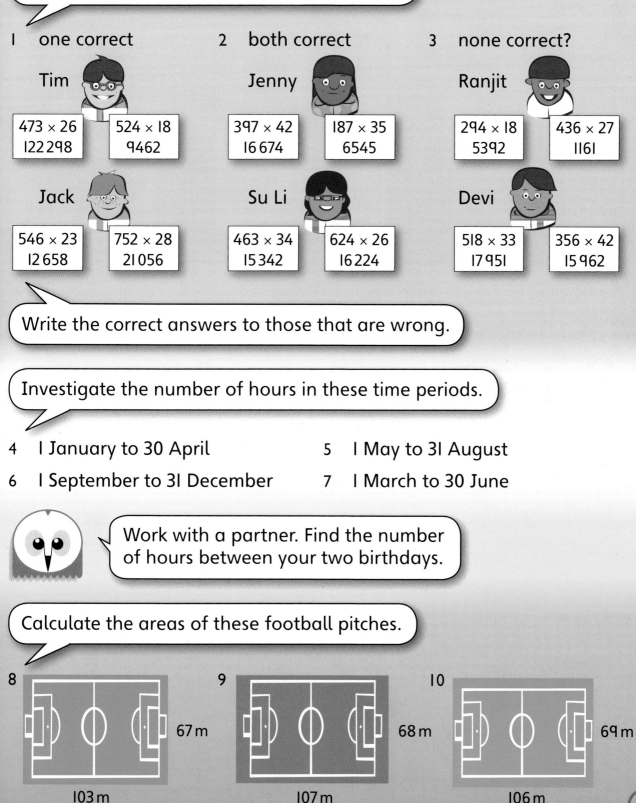

8 67 m / 103 m

9 68 m / 107 m

10 69 m / 106 m

13

Multiplying

Calculate the areas of these table tops.

1.
```
    6 0 0 0
      1 3 8
  ×    6 4
  _____
  _____
```

1
64 cm
138 cm

2
32 cm
154 cm

3
43 cm
183 cm

4
48 cm
247 cm

5
54 cm
221 cm

6
58 cm
109 cm

7
82 cm
237 cm

Explore

Use these digit cards: **3** **4** **5** **6** **7**

Create a multiplication like this: ☐☐☐ × ☐☐

Investigate which arrangement gives the smallest possible answer.

Which gives the greatest possible answer?

8 Last month the store sold 18 washing machines at £324 each and 21 dishwashers at £426 each. How much did they take altogether for these two items?

9 It is 132 miles from London to Sheffield. Neelaksh makes 18 return trips in a year. How far has he travelled?

Multiplying decimals

Copy and complete.

1 7 × 4·3
   (28)
   7 × 4   = 28
   7 × 0·3 = 2·1
   _____
   7 × 4·3 =

2 8 × 5·2
   (40)
   8 × 5   = 40
   8 × 0·2 =
   _____
   8 × 5·2 =

3 4 × 3·6
   ( )
   4 × 3   = 12
   4 × 0·6 =
   _____
   4 × 3·6 =

4 3 × 5·8

5 9 × 6·4

6 6 × 7·8

7 4 × 2·9

8 3 × 7·7

9 5 × 4·6

10 3 × 6·3

11 5 × 2·8

12 4 × 5·4

13 3 × 6·6

14 5 × 3·7

15 4 × 4·3

These children recorded how long it took to write their name. How long do they take to write their name the given number of times?

16. 8 × 2·7
    (24)
    8 × 2   = ...
    8 × 0·7 = ...
    8 × 2·7 = ...

16 Guy
    2·7 seconds
    8 times

17 Tracey
    5·6 seconds
    4 times

18 Catherine
    9·2 seconds
    7 times

19 Ilesh
    6·4 seconds
    5 times

20 Elizabeth
    9·4 seconds
    6 times

21 Davinder
    8·7 seconds
    3 times

22 Tim
    1·9 seconds
    7 times

23 Sunam
    4·7 seconds
    6 times

24 Yasmin
    7·3 seconds
    4 times

Work with a partner. Use a stopwatch to find how long it takes to write your name and address. Use multiplication to find how long it would take to write it 12 times.

Multiplying decimals

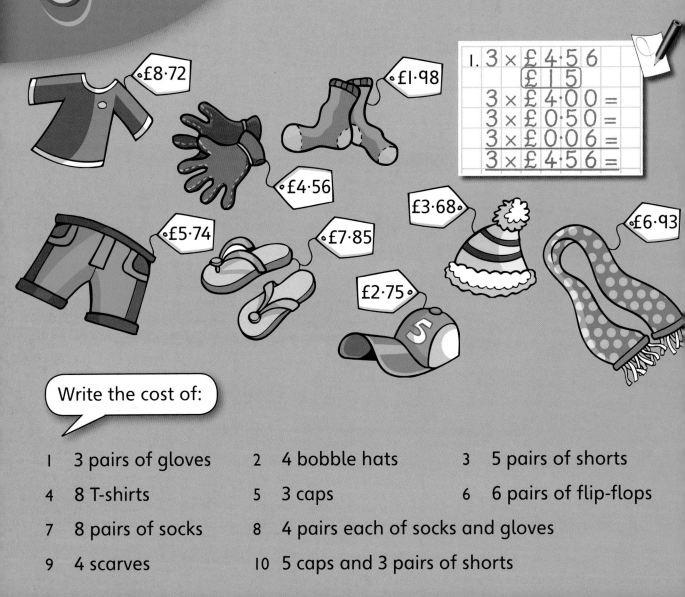

£8·72 £1·98 £4·56 £5·74 £7·85 £3·68 £6·93 £2·75

1. 3 × £4·56
£15
3 × £4·00 =
3 × £0·50 =
3 × £0·06 =
3 × £4·56 =

Write the cost of:

1   3 pairs of gloves

2   4 bobble hats

3   5 pairs of shorts

4   8 T-shirts

5   3 caps

6   6 pairs of flip-flops

7   8 pairs of socks

8   4 pairs each of socks and gloves

9   4 scarves

10 5 caps and 3 pairs of shorts

You can buy any two items. Investigate how many of each you can buy with £30.

Complete these multiplications.

11 3 × 1·26

12 4 × 2·57

13 5 × 4·36

14 8 × 7·42

15 9 × 3·87

16 4 × 8·64

17 7 × 3·92

18 6 × 4·38

19 9 × 5·28

Multiplying decimals

Nine children created a decimal multiplication. Whose answer is nearest to 20? Whose is second nearest?

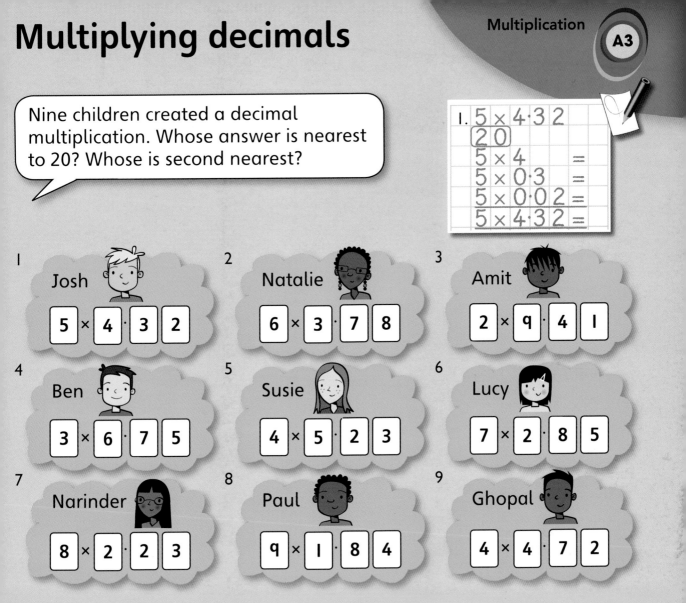

1. $5 \times 4\cdot32$
   20
   5×4 =
   $5 \times 0\cdot3$ =
   $5 \times 0\cdot02$ =
   $5 \times 4\cdot32$ =

1 Josh
| 5 | × | 4 | . | 3 | 2 |

2 Natalie
| 6 | × | 3 | . | 7 | 8 |

3 Amit
| 2 | × | 9 | . | 4 | 1 |

4 Ben
| 3 | × | 6 | . | 7 | 5 |

5 Susie
| 4 | × | 5 | . | 2 | 3 |

6 Lucy
| 7 | × | 2 | . | 8 | 5 |

7 Narinder
| 8 | × | 2 | . | 2 | 3 |

8 Paul
| 9 | × | 1 | . | 8 | 4 |

9 Ghopal
| 4 | × | 4 | . | 7 | 2 |

Calculate the perimeters of these regular polygons.

10 a square of side 3·24 cm

11 a pentagon of side 4·56 cm

12 an octagon of side 5·73 cm

13 an equilateral triangle of side 9·28 cm

14 a hexagon of side 4·47 cm

15 a nonagon of side 6·83 cm

16 a hexagon of side 8·67 cm

17 an octagon of side 6·84 cm

18 a pentagon of side 7·68 cm

19 a square of side 6·37 cm

A shape shop sells plastic regular polygons. All the sides of the polygons are 3·69 cm long. Investigate the perimeter of the different polygons.

Multiplying decimals

Choose three of the four digits to make the multiplication correct.

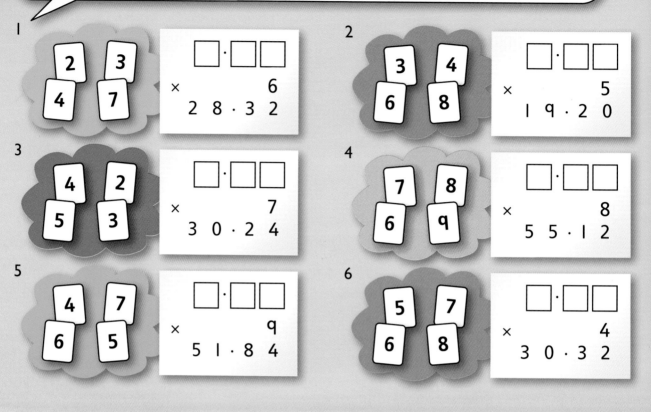

1.
```
[2] [3]
[4] [7]
```
$$\square . \square \square$$
$$\times \qquad 6$$
$$\overline{2\ 8 \cdot 3\ 2}$$

2.
```
[3] [4]
[6] [8]
```
$$\square . \square \square$$
$$\times \qquad 5$$
$$\overline{1\ 9 \cdot 2\ 0}$$

3.
```
[4] [2]
[5] [3]
```
$$\square . \square \square$$
$$\times \qquad 7$$
$$\overline{3\ 0 \cdot 2\ 4}$$

4.
```
[7] [8]
[6] [9]
```
$$\square . \square \square$$
$$\times \qquad 8$$
$$\overline{5\ 5 \cdot 1\ 2}$$

5.
```
[4] [7]
[6] [5]
```
$$\square . \square \square$$
$$\times \qquad 9$$
$$\overline{5\ 1 \cdot 8\ 4}$$

6.
```
[5] [7]
[6] [8]
```
$$\square . \square \square$$
$$\times \qquad 4$$
$$\overline{3\ 0 \cdot 3\ 2}$$

 **Explore**

$3 \cdot 27 \times 4 = 6 \cdot 54 \times 2$

Can you find other pairs of multiplications like this: $\square . \square \square \times \square$ that have the same answer?

7   Jim has 8 pieces of fencing, each 1·86 m long. He needs to build a fence 20 m long. How short is his fence, and how many more pieces must he buy?

8   Rashida buys a fish tank for £35·70 and 8 fish at £2·76 each. She only has £45·30 in her purse. How much more will she need to borrow?

9   Kate and 6 of her friends are going on a train journey. The tickets cost £6·38 each. How much change will they have from £50?

Adding

> Copy and complete.

```
1.  ⑦
    3·3 2
  + 4·1 8
    7·5 0
      1
```

1.   3·32
    + 4·18
    ──────

2.   6·72
    + 3·84
    ──────

3.   4·63
    + 2·58
    ──────

4.   5·44
    + 2·83
    ──────

5.   3·67
    + 2·25
    ──────

6.   4·32
    + 3·84
    ──────

7.   6·47
    + 1·25
    ──────

8.   4·58
    + 5·24
    ──────

9.   4·31
    + 2·93
    ──────

10.   5·36
     + 1·29
    ──────

11.   3·87
     + 2·62
    ──────

> Write the total quantity.

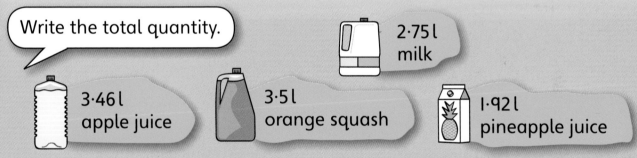

3·46 l
apple juice

3·5 l
orange squash

2·75 l
milk

1·92 l
pineapple juice

2·09 l
lemon squash

12   apple juice and milk

13   pineapple juice, lemon squash, orange squash

14   milk and lemon squash

15   apple juice, pineapple juice, orange squash

16   lemon squash, orange squash

17   orange squash, lemon squash, milk

> How many ways are there of filling in these
> missing numbers? 3·☐6 + 1·☐☐ = 5

Adding

Copy and complete.

1   5·06 + 3·7 + 2·85

2   6·72 + 3·85

3   4·8 + 2·05 + 0·87

4   2·68 + 4·93 + 1·76

5   5·76 + 3·8

6   5·36 + 4·4 + 3·12

7   3·57 + 8·2 + 7·4

8   6·18 + 3·12

```
1.    12
      5·06
      3·7
    + 2·85
    ──────
     11·61
      1 1
```

Add the weights of the bags.

```
9.    1 6
      5·72
      6·84
    + 3·25
    ──────
     15·81 kg
      1 1
```

9
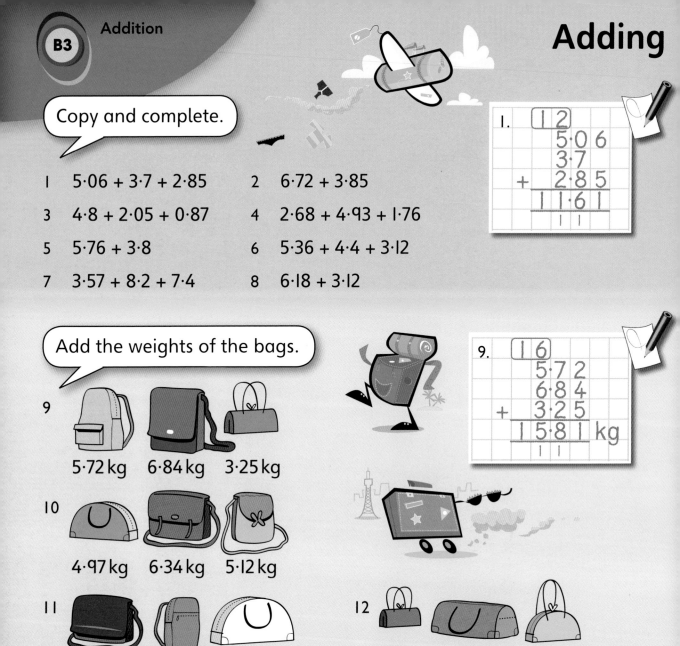

5·72 kg   6·84 kg   3·25 kg

10
4·97 kg   6·34 kg   5·12 kg

11
6·79 kg   4·38 kg   7·84 kg

12
2·89 kg   6·38 kg   4·64 kg

13
5·64 kg   7·92 kg   4·18 kg

14
3·64 kg   4·93 kg   5·78 kg

15
3·84 kg   6·47 kg   5·32 kg

16
2·37 kg   7·26 kg   1·19 kg

The luggage limit is 20 kg. How much more can each passenger carry?

Adding

£28·73

Tombola

£15·17

Teas

£15·30

Splat the Rat

£7·08

Weight of the Cake

£32·09

White Elephant

£27·49

Greasy Pole

£3·50

Hoop-lah

After a village fair the takings are added. Write the totals for:

1. White Elephant, Hoop-lah and Splat the Rat

2. Tombola, Greasy Pole, Weight of the Cake and Teas

3. White Elephant, Splat the Rat and Weight of the Cake

4. Tombola, Greasy Pole, Hoop-lah and Teas

5. Teas, Splat the rat, Tombola and Greasy Pole

6. White Elephant, Greasy Pole and Tombola

7. Weight of the cake, Hoop-lah, Teas and Tombola

8. Splat the Rat, Weight of the Cake, White Elephant and Hoop-lah

9. Three cakes weigh 3·75 kg, 2·18 kg and 1·9 kg. Find their total weight on the cake stall.

10. Shola buys a brass teapot (£4·45) a hat stand (£5·69) and an egg beater (85p). How much does she pay the White Elephant stall? How much change does she get from £20?

11. Jim spends £2·87 on the Tombola, £1·75 on the Hoop-lah and 76p climbing the Greasy Pole. How much does he spend in total?

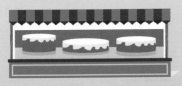

Write your own word problem set at the village

Adding

Copy and complete.

1   5·07 + 0·65 + 1·8

2   3·75 + 4·86 + 0·07

3   4·08 + 3·9 + 4·24

4   1·4 + 3·65 + 0·795

5   6·3 + 4·098 + 3·27

6   6·09 + 1·8 + 4·067

7   5·1 + 3·7 + 6·08

8   3·286 + 7·07 + 2·8

Explore

☐·☐☐ + ☐·☐☐ + ☐·☐☐ = 10

Find some ways of filling the boxes, e.g. 2·53 + 3·12 + 4·35 = 10

Can you find some ways in which no digit is used more than once?

True or false?

10
Adding three 2-place decimal numbers always results in an answer greater than 4.

11
Three lots of £1·99 is equal to twice £2·99.

9
1·23 + 4·56 is one half of 6·54 + 3·21.

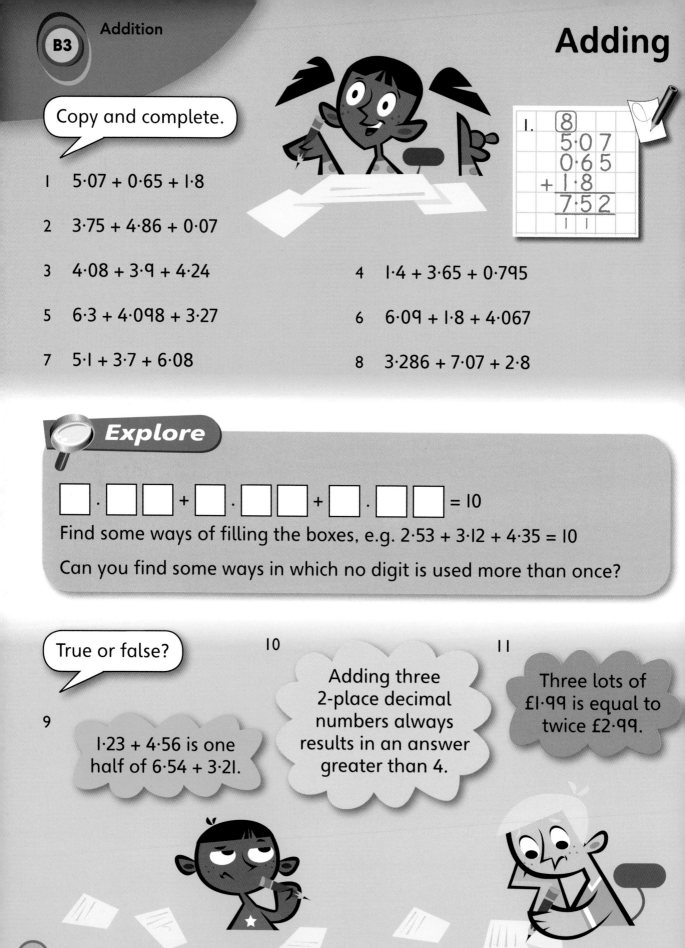

Subtracting

> Subtract the smaller from the larger number.

```
1.   3 0 0 0
         2 1
       5 4 3 2
     - 2 1 1 8
       3 3 1 4
```

1   5432 – 2118

2   4826 – 1452

3   6128 – 4029

4   7269 – 3542

5   7636 – 2172

6   6583 – 4128

7   5296 – 2734

8   4831 – 3614

> Write the difference between the two distances.

```
9.   1 5 0 0
       2 1
     3 1 7 5
   - 1 4 3 2
     1 7 4 3 km
```

9   3175 km   1432 km

10 5647 km   2518 km

11 4361 km   9628 km

12 8496 km   3753 km

13 3271 km   7632 km

14 2219 km   9438 km

15 5296 km   2534 km

16 5272 km   8635 km

> Arrange the digits 1–8 in this calculation:
>
> □ □ □ □ – □ □ □ □ =
>
> to give the largest possible answer.

Subtracting

Write the difference between the two amounts.

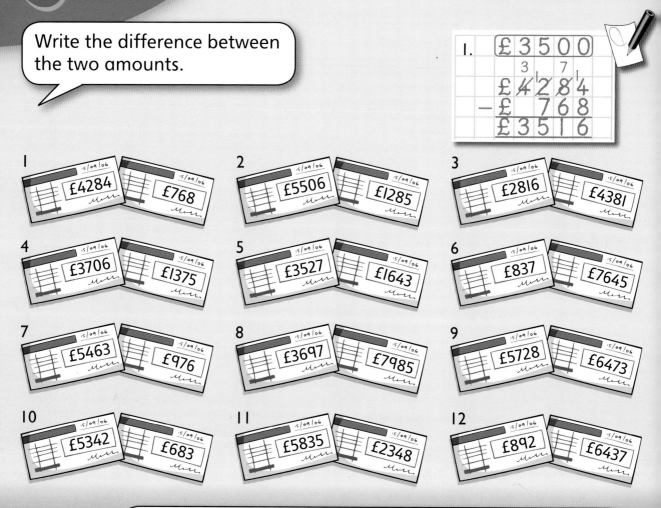

1.
£3500
  3   7
£4284
− £ 768
£3516

1. £4284   £768

2. £5506   £1285

3. £2816   £4381

4. £3706   £1375

5. £3527   £1643

6. £837   £7645

7. £5463   £976

8. £3697   £7985

9. £5728   £6473

10. £5342   £683

11. £5835   £2348

12. £892   £6437

Work with a partner. Choose two of the additions each. Check your partner's answers by adding the answer to the smaller number.

Copy and complete.

13   53146
   −   2817
   _____

14   3881
   − 1976
   _____

15   64378
   −   2769
   _____

16   5436
   − 1787
   _____

17   33265
   −   1678
   _____

18   6384
   − 2637
   _____

Subtracting

> Find the difference between the length and the width of each rug.

1.
```
  1500
  2 4
  3 5̶ 4̶ 8
 - 1 8 6 2
   1 6 8 6 mm
```

1

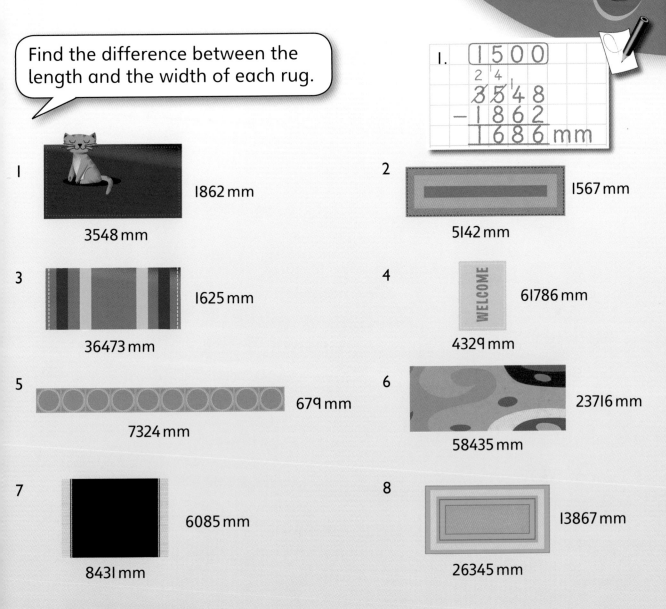

1862 mm

3548 mm

2

1567 mm

5142 mm

3

1625 mm

36473 mm

4

WELCOME

61786 mm

4329 mm

5

679 mm

7324 mm

6

23716 mm

58435 mm

7

6085 mm

8431 mm

8

13867 mm

26345 mm

Explore

Write two numbers with consecutive digits, e.g. 7654 and 345.

Reverse the digits: 4567 and 543.

Subtract the smaller number from the larger.
Try two different numbers with consecutive digits. Look for patterns.

What happens if you include 0?

What about 5-digit numbers?

Subtracting

Write the difference between the mountain heights.

Mont Blanc	Eiger	Matterhorn	Weisshorn	Silberhorn
4810 m	3974 m	4478 m	4505 m	3695 m

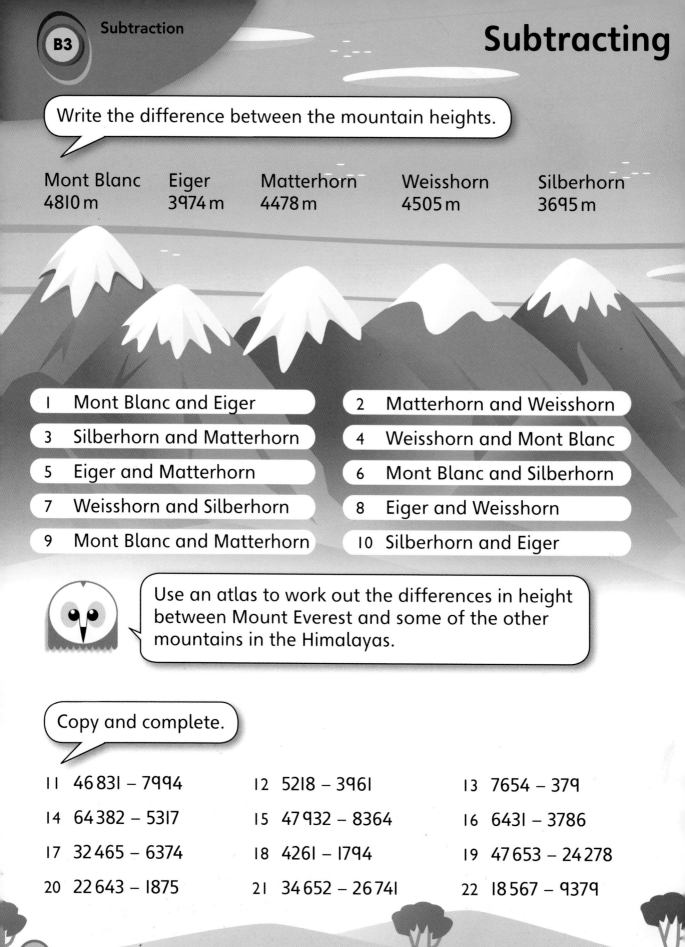

1   Mont Blanc and Eiger

2   Matterhorn and Weisshorn

3   Silberhorn and Matterhorn

4   Weisshorn and Mont Blanc

5   Eiger and Matterhorn

6   Mont Blanc and Silberhorn

7   Weisshorn and Silberhorn

8   Eiger and Weisshorn

9   Mont Blanc and Matterhorn

10   Silberhorn and Eiger

Use an atlas to work out the differences in height between Mount Everest and some of the other mountains in the Himalayas.

Copy and complete.

11 46 831 – 7994

12 5218 – 3961

13 7654 – 379

14 64 382 – 5317

15 47 932 – 8364

16 6431 – 3786

17 32 465 – 6374

18 4261 – 1794

19 47 653 – 24 278

20 22 643 – 1875

21 34 652 – 26 741

22 18 567 – 9379

Subtracting

> Complete each subtraction.

1   4·38 – 2·55

2   6·72 – 4·38

3   6·52 – 1·91

4   7·64 – 3·73

5   8·62 – 3·49

6   6·43 – 4·82

7   6·33 – 1·28

8   6·38 – 2·74

9   7·24 – 4·33

10 5·62 – 2·37

```
1.    2
      3
     4̶ˌ3 8
    – 2ˌ5 5
      1ˌ8 3
```

> ☐·36 – 2·☐1 = 1·85. Find the possible missing numbers.

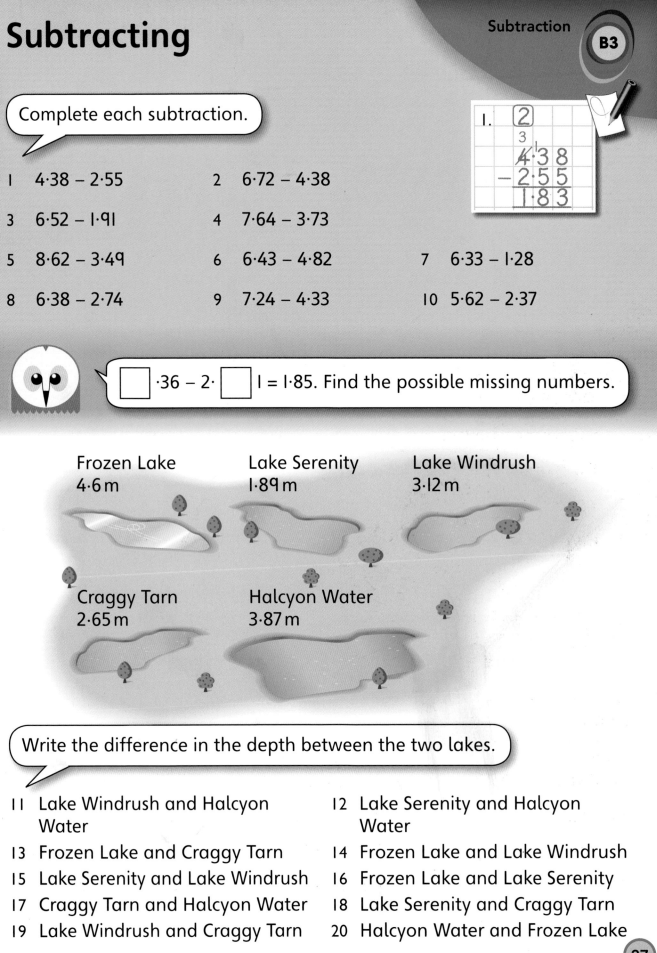

Frozen Lake
4·6 m

Lake Serenity
1·89 m

Lake Windrush
3·12 m

Craggy Tarn
2·65 m

Halcyon Water
3·87 m

> Write the difference in the depth between the two lakes.

11 Lake Windrush and Halcyon Water

12 Lake Serenity and Halcyon Water

13 Frozen Lake and Craggy Tarn

14 Frozen Lake and Lake Windrush

15 Lake Serenity and Lake Windrush

16 Frozen Lake and Lake Serenity

17 Craggy Tarn and Halcyon Water

18 Lake Serenity and Craggy Tarn

19 Lake Windrush and Craggy Tarn

20 Halcyon Water and Frozen Lake

Subtracting

Find the difference between each pair of children's savings.

1.

	£	6			
£	1	1	·	3	8
− £		4	·	8	6

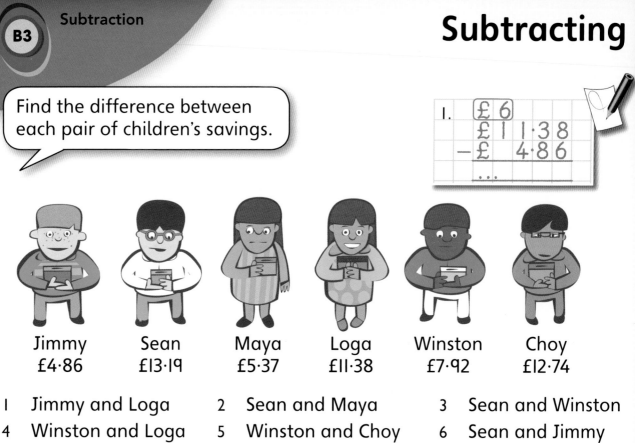

Jimmy £4·86   Sean £13·19   Maya £5·37   Loga £11·38   Winston £7·92   Choy £12·74

1 Jimmy and Loga   2 Sean and Maya   3 Sean and Winston
4 Winston and Loga   5 Winston and Choy   6 Sean and Jimmy
7 Maya and Jimmy   8 Winston and Jimmy   9 Loga and Choy
10 Loga and Maya

Use digits 1–9. Create a ☐ · ☐ ☐ − ☐ · ☐ ☐ calculation that has an answer as close as possible to 5.

Write the amount left to

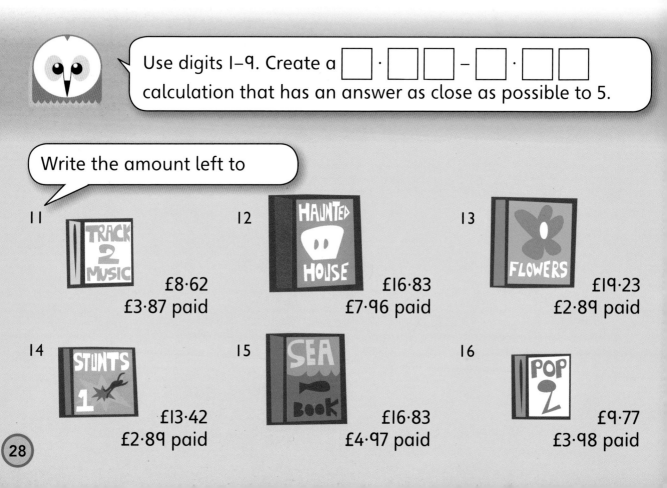

11 £8·62   £3·87 paid

12 HAUNTED HOUSE   £16·83   £7·96 paid

13 FLOWERS   £19·23   £2·89 paid

14 STUNTS 1   £13·42   £2·89 paid

15 SEA BOOK   £16·83   £4·97 paid

16 POP 2   £9·77   £3·98 paid

28

Subtracting

Some water runs out of each pool. Write the number of litres left.

1.
$$
\begin{array}{r}
7\,7 \\
7\;\overset{5}{6} \\
8\,6\cdot7\,0 \\
-\quad\ 9\cdot8\,3 \\
\hline
7\,6\cdot8\,7\ \text{litres}
\end{array}
$$

1 **86·7l**
9·83l runs out

2 **26·5l**
8·75l runs out

3 **57·3l**
6·92l runs out

4 **62·4l**
3·71l runs out

5 **74·5l**
7·84l runs out

6 **46·3l**
9·87l runs out

7 **63·2l**
7·64l runs out

8 **55·4l**
8·63l runs out

Look at these subtractions. Find the common mistake, then write the correct subtraction.

$$
\begin{array}{r}
2\cdot74 \\
-\ 1\cdot36 \\
\hline
1\cdot42
\end{array}
\qquad
\begin{array}{r}
3\cdot17 \\
-\ 1\cdot54 \\
\hline
2\cdot43
\end{array}
$$

9 Sunil had saved £86·50. He spent £9·32 on a meal and £4·80 on a cinema ticket. How much did he have left?

10 A pipeline ran 82·3 metres from a tank to the house. If all except 17·85 m has to be replaced, how many metres is that?

11 Rover's owner buys a 6·8 kg bag of dog food. In the first week he eats 1·2 kg of food, and the week after that he eats 1·68 kg. How much is left in the bag?

MUTT

Subtracting

Find the weight of letters left in the postman's bag after 1 hour.

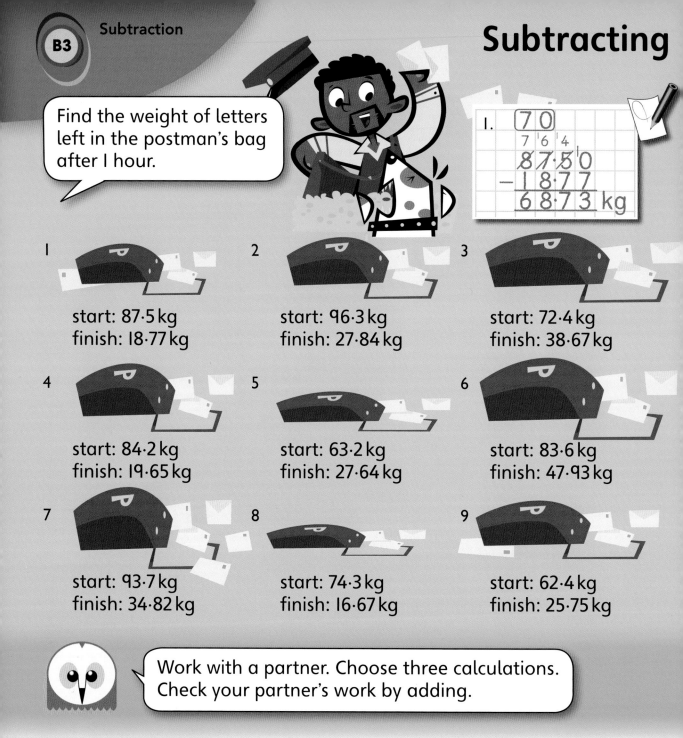

1.
```
    ⁷0
  7 ⁶1⁴
  8 7·5 0
- 1 8·7 7
  6 8·7 3 kg
```

1
start: 87·5 kg
finish: 18·77 kg

2
start: 96·3 kg
finish: 27·84 kg

3
start: 72·4 kg
finish: 38·67 kg

4
start: 84·2 kg
finish: 19·65 kg

5
start: 63·2 kg
finish: 27·64 kg

6
start: 83·6 kg
finish: 47·93 kg

7
start: 93·7 kg
finish: 34·82 kg

8
start: 74·3 kg
finish: 16·67 kg

9
start: 62·4 kg
finish: 25·75 kg

Work with a partner. Choose three calculations. Check your partner's work by adding.

Explore

Start with a 2-decimal place number with repeating digits, e.g. 54·54.

Subtract a 2-decimal place number, also with repeating digits, e.g. 27·27.

Look at the answer.

Repeat this process – look for different patterns.

Capacity

Write each quantity in litres.

1. 70 cl = 0.7 litres

1 70 cl

2 300 ml

3 5 ml

4 20 000 ml

5 400 ml

6 90 cl

7 3000 ml

8 4 ml

Write each quantity in millilitres.

9. 1.5 l = 1500 ml

9 1.5 l

10 0.55 l

11 500 cl

12 2.5 l

13 0.65 l

14 750 cl

15 4 l

16 1.75 l

Write the units you would use to measure:

17. millilitres

17 a bottle of shampoo

18 the petrol in a car

19 the water in a bath

20 the medicine in a spoon

21 the yolk in an egg

22 the milk in a carton

23 the fizzy pop in a can

24 the toothpaste in a tube

25 the juice in a jug

How many medicine spoons (5 ml) do you think it would take to fill a bath (150 litres)? Now work it out!

Capacity

2·2 gallons = 10 litres
1 gallon = 4·5 litres

1. 40 litres = 8·8 gallons

Write the capacity of each car in gallons.

1 40 litres

2 100 litres

3 18 litres

4 90 litres

5 45 litres

6 5 litres

7 20 litres

8 27 litres

9 30 litres

A garage sells petrol at £1·18 per litre. Work with a partner to find the cost per gallon. If you were the garage, which price would you advertise?

Write the amount of milk in litres.

1 pint = 0·56 litres
1 litre = 1·75 pints

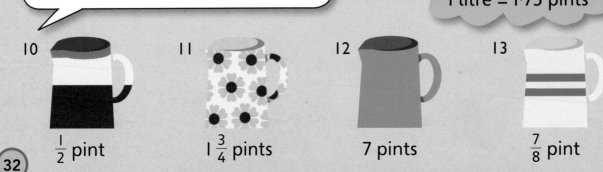

10 $\frac{1}{2}$ pint

11 $1\frac{3}{4}$ pints

12 7 pints

13 $\frac{7}{8}$ pint

Capacity

Use the scale to complete the equivalences to the nearest tenth.

1. 15 litres $=$
   $3\cdot5$ gallons

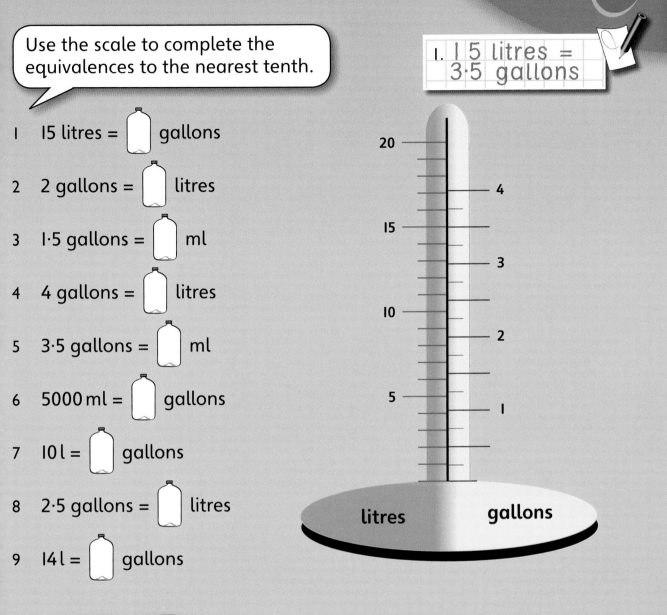

1 15 litres = ☐ gallons

2 2 gallons = ☐ litres

3 1·5 gallons = ☐ ml

4 4 gallons = ☐ litres

5 3·5 gallons = ☐ ml

6 5000 ml = ☐ gallons

7 10 l = ☐ gallons

8 2·5 gallons = ☐ litres

9 14 l = ☐ gallons

litres   gallons

Explore

Imagine that England and Wales went back to working in pints!

Look at and consider as many bottles and containers as possible.

Re-write their capacity in pints.

Orange juice   juice

2 litres

Fizzy cola

1 litre

Probability

no chance   even chance   certain

0      $\frac{1}{2}$ 1

Say if the chance of these events happening is:

- less than even
- more than even
- certain
- no chance
- even chance

1. less than even

1 throwing a 6 on a dice

2 a coin landing heads

3 a dice landing on a number greater than 3

4 a card from a pack being red

5 a coin landing heads or tails

7 a card from a pack being black

6 a card from a pack being a spade

8 a dice landing on a number less than 6

9 a card from a pack being hearts or clubs

10 a dice landing on a 2 or 4

Explore

Use an 8-sided dice (numbered 1–8). Write an event that matches each of these: less than even, more than even, certain, no chance, even.

Probability

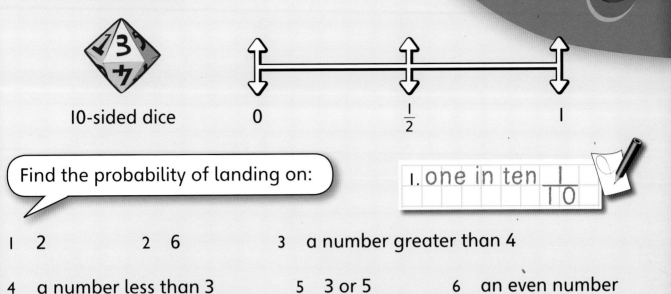

10-sided dice   0 $\frac{1}{2}$ 1

Find the probability of landing on:

1. one in ten $\frac{1}{10}$

| 1 2 | 2 6 | 3 a number greater than 4 |

4   a number less than 3   5   3 or 5   6   an even number

7   a number greater than 10   8   an odd number

9   a square number   10   an odd number greater than 2

11   an even number less than 5   12   a prime number

True or false?

13   You are less likely to draw a red card than a black card from a pack of cards.

14   The probability of throwing a 6 on a dice is less than the probability of throwing a 1.

15   The chance of taking a picture card from a pack is greater than $\frac{1}{2}$.

16   A probability of $\frac{4}{9}$ is less than an even chance.

Discuss whether it is more likely that an adult will be the next person to enter the classroom than a child.

Probability

In Amit's video collection
1 out of 10 films is a romance,
3 out of 10 are comedy,
4 out of 10 are cartoons and
2 out of 10 are action.

What is the probability of taking these films:

1   comedy   2   action   3   romance   4   cartoon

5   a comedy or a cartoon   6   a romance or a comedy

7   an action or a comedy   8   not a romance

9   not a comedy   10   neither a comedy nor a cartoon

11   neither a romance, action, comedy nor a cartoon?

 If 1 out of 12 is a thriller, 4 out of 12 are horrors, 5 out of 12 are science fiction, and 2 out of 12 are cartoons, invent some events that have more than an even chance of happening.

Explore

You have cards 1–10.

Taking a card at random, what is the probability that it is a prime number?

Now imagine you have cards 1–20, 1–30, 1–40, 1–50, etc.

Probability

You have a pack of playing cards with no picture cards.
Write the probability that a card you take is:

1. $\frac{1}{2}$

1 red

2 a spade

3 a heart

4 a spade or a heart

5 less than 5

6 a red 10

7 a black card greater than 6

8 a red even card

9 a diamond or a heart

10 a black 7

11 a black odd card

12 greater than 10

13 not a heart

14 between 4 and 7

15 3 of clubs

16 not red

17 a prime number

18 neither red nor black

19 black and even

20 an odd heart

21 a six

22 a red 7

Explore

You have a set of number cards 1–20.

The probability of taking a card less than 11 is $\frac{1}{2}$.

Think of events to match these probabilities.

23 $\frac{1}{4}$ 24 1   25 $\frac{1}{5}$ 26 0   27 $\frac{3}{20}$

Pie charts

Car colour

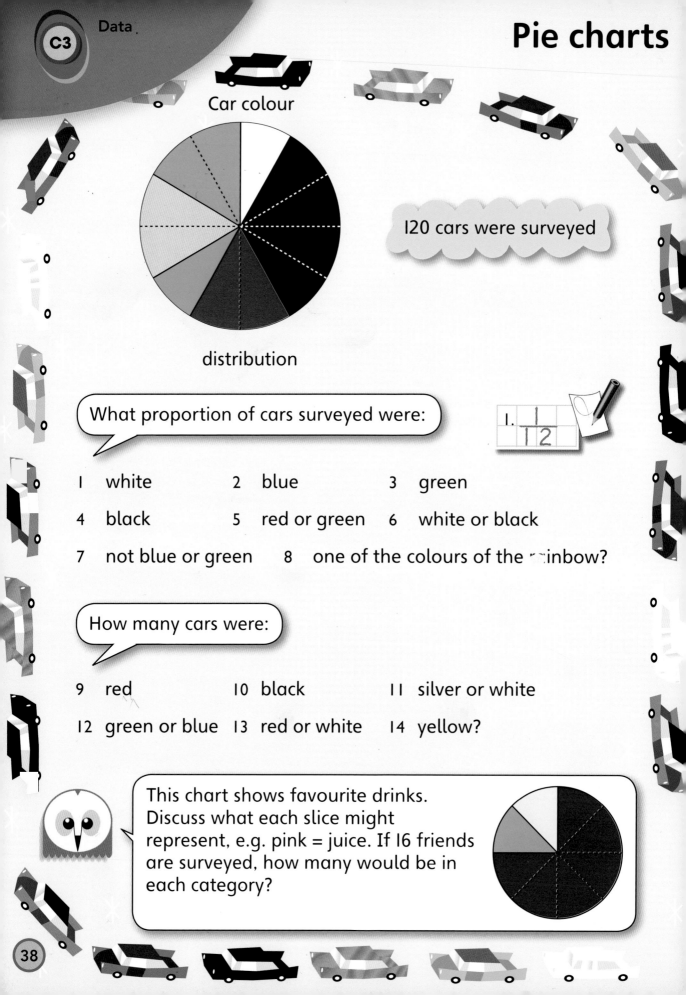

distribution

120 cars were surveyed

What proportion of cars surveyed were:

1. $\frac{1}{12}$

1	white	2 blue	3 green

1   white   2   blue   3   green

4   black   5   red or green   6   white or black

7   not blue or green   8   one of the colours of the rainbow?

How many cars were:

9   red   10 black   11 silver or white

12 green or blue   13 red or white   14 yellow?

This chart shows favourite drinks. Discuss what each slice might represent, e.g. pink = juice. If 16 friends are surveyed, how many would be in each category?

Pie charts

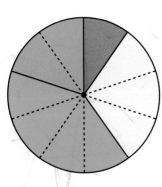

Dinosaur
Nineteen
Music
Hairbrush
Smooth
Shop
Toothpaste

Diplodocus
Fin
Cake
Poster
Friend
Sandwich
Machine

Aardvark
Bluebell
Nonsense
Caterpillars
Wheelbarrows
Pit

Word length	1–3	4–6	7–9	10–12
Number of words				

Which slice could represent words with these numbers of letters?

1. pink

1   1–3   2   4–6   3   7–9   4   10–12

How many words have:

5   fewer than 6 letters   6   more than 10 letters

7   between 4 and 12 letters   8   1–3 letters

9   more than 7 letters   10 between 10 and 12 letters?

Explore

Write 16 words to fit this pie chart.

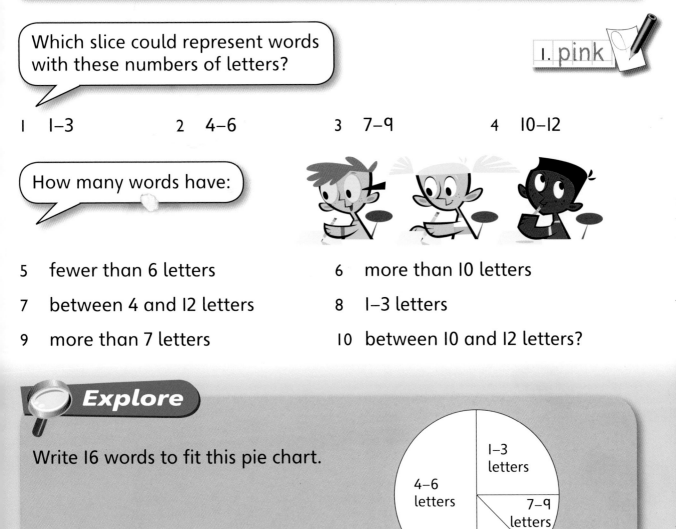

1–3 letters

4–6 letters

7–9 letters

10–12 letters

Pie charts

Car nationality

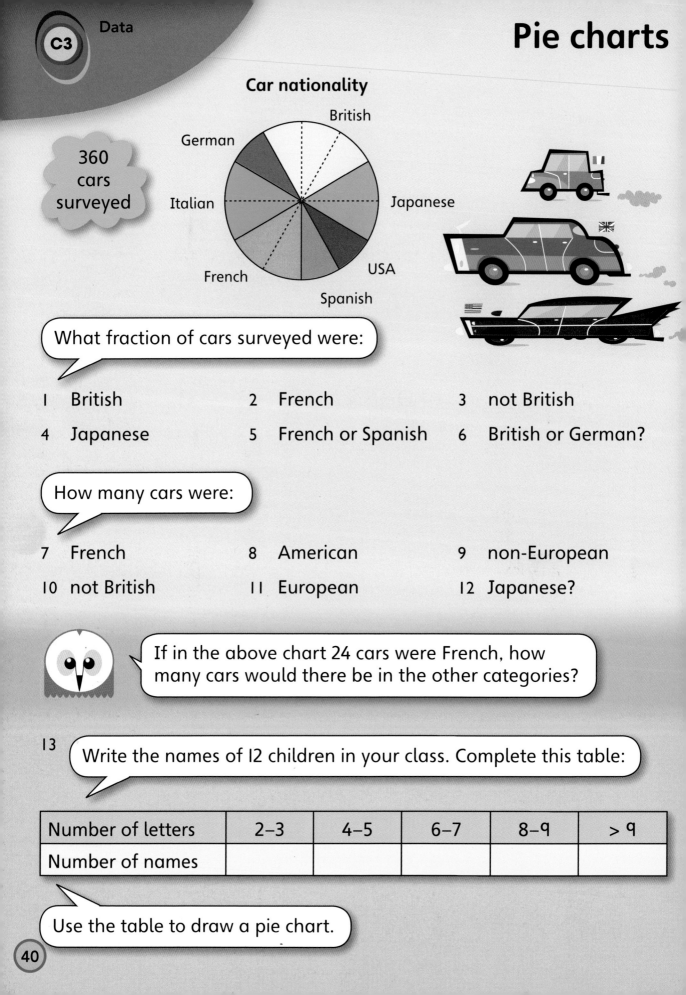

360 cars surveyed

What fraction of cars surveyed were:

1 British

2 French

3 not British

4 Japanese

5 French or Spanish

6 British or German?

How many cars were:

7 French

8 American

9 non-European

10 not British

11 European

12 Japanese?

If in the above chart 24 cars were French, how many cars would there be in the other categories?

13 Write the names of 12 children in your class. Complete this table:

Number of letters	2–3	4–5	6–7	8–9	> 9
Number of names					

Use the table to draw a pie chart.

Pie charts

Types of homes

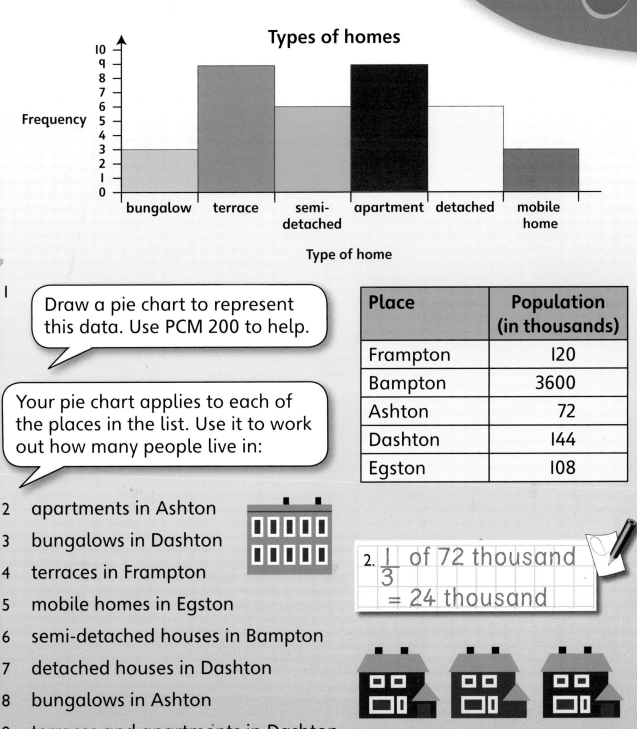

Frequency

bungalow   terrace   semi-detached   apartment   detached   mobile home

Type of home

1   Draw a pie chart to represent this data. Use PCM 200 to help.

Your pie chart applies to each of the places in the list. Use it to work out how many people live in:

Place	Population (in thousands)
Frampton	120
Bampton	3600
Ashton	72
Dashton	144
Egston	108

2   apartments in Ashton

3   bungalows in Dashton

4   terraces in Frampton

5   mobile homes in Egston

6   semi-detached houses in Bampton

7   detached houses in Dashton

8   bungalows in Ashton

9   terraces and apartments in Dashton

10   semi-detached and detached houses in Frampton

2. $\frac{1}{3}$ of 72 thousand
    = 24 thousand

How would the pie chart look in your area?

41

Perimeter

```
1. 22 + 27 = 49 cm
   49 × 2 = 98 cm
   0·98 m
```

Write the perimeter of each picture in metres.

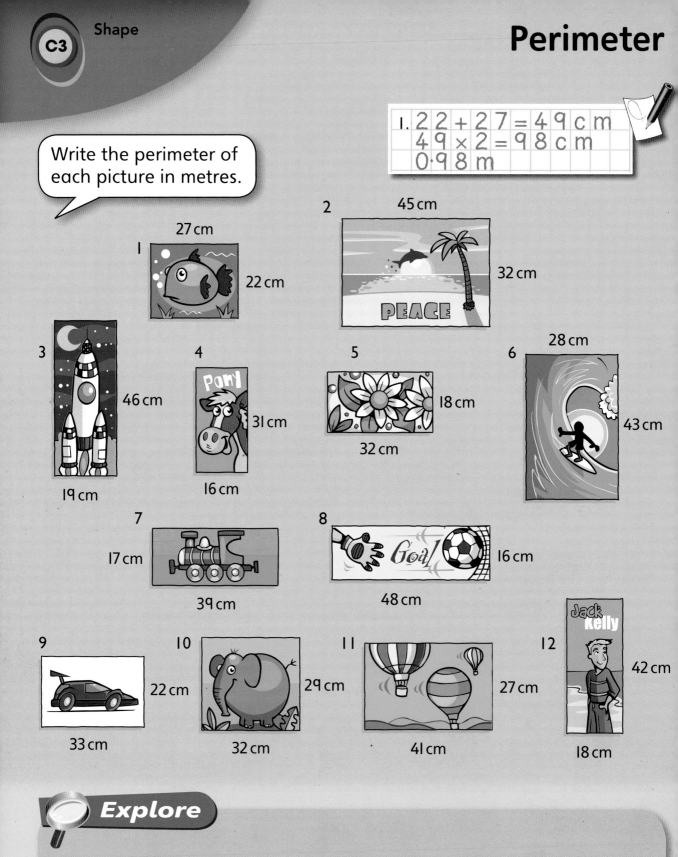

1   27 cm   22 cm

2   45 cm   32 cm

3   46 cm   19 cm

4   Pony   31 cm   16 cm

5   18 cm   32 cm

6   28 cm   43 cm

7   17 cm   39 cm

8   Goal   48 cm   16 cm

9   22 cm   33 cm

10   29 cm   32 cm

11   27 cm   41 cm

12   Jack Kelly   42 cm   18 cm

Explore

Draw three rectangles with a perimeter of 12 units.
Draw another with the same perimeter where the sides are not a whole number of squares.

Perimeter

Each set of cards is being given a gold edge. Work out the perimeter of each card.

1. $3·5 + 4·8 = 8·3$
   $2 × 8·3 = 16·6$ cm

1 3·5 cm
8 cm

2 4·2 cm
5·6 cm

3 5·1 cm
6·4 cm

4 4·3 cm
7·5 cm

5 4·2 cm
3·5 cm

6 3·6 cm
2·2 cm

7 5·1 cm
3·6 cm

8 7·3 cm
4·4 cm

True or false: there are seven ways of drawing a rectangle with a perimeter of 30 cm.

Find the difference between the perimeter of the inside and outside of the picture frames.

9. $16 + 8 = 24$ cm
   $24 × 2 = 48$ cm
   $16 − 4 = 12$ cm
   $8 − 4 = 4$ cm
   $12 + 4 = 16$ cm
   $16 × 2 = 32$ cm
   Difference $= 16$ cm

9 8 cm
2 cm
6 cm
2 cm

10 13 cm
18 cm
3 cm
3 cm

11 12 cm
8 cm
2 cm
2 cm

Investigate which frames have the largest and smallest areas.

43

Perimeter

Write the perimeter of each games mat in metres.

1. P = 14 + 12 + ...

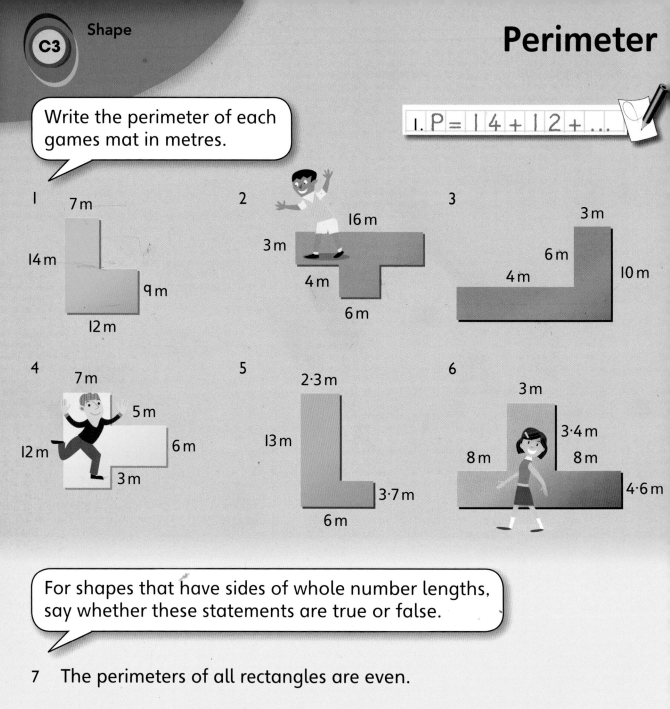

For shapes that have sides of whole number lengths, say whether these statements are true or false.

7   The perimeters of all rectangles are even.

8   All squares have a perimeter that will divide exactly by 4.

9   Two sides of a rectangle are double the length of the other two sides. The perimeter could be 18 cm.

10 A rectangle where one side is 1 cm can have a perimeter of 19 cm.

Explore areas of shapes that have a perimeter of 36 cm.

Perimeter

Explore

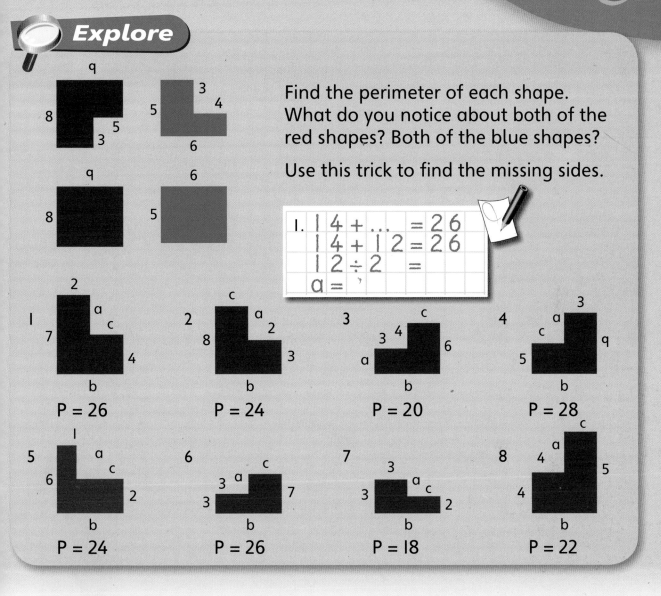

Find the perimeter of each shape. What do you notice about both of the red shapes? Both of the blue shapes?

Use this trick to find the missing sides.

1. 14 + ... = 26
   14 + 12 = 26
   12 ÷ 2 =
   a =

P = 26

P = 24

P = 20

P = 28

P = 24

P = 26

P = 18

P = 22

9   Tim had a rectangular plot of allotment. One side was 12·5 m and the perimeter was 43 m. What was the other side?

10 True or false? A rectangular garden with a perimeter of 50 m cannot have a side of 25 metres.

11 What is the perimeter of a rectangular tile whose shorter side is 2·5 cm shorter than the longer side of 4·6 cm?

12 Side A = Side B^2. The perimeter is 24 cm. What are the lengths of the sides of the rectangle?

Time

Complete each sentence.

1   3 days = ☐ hours

2   5 minutes = ☐ seconds

3   4 decades = ☐ years

4   ☐ days = 2 fortnights

5   104 weeks = ☐ years

6   5 decades = ☐ century

7   3 years = ☐ weeks

8   4 hours = ☐ minutes

9   ☐ minutes = 10 hours

10   12 hours = ☐ seconds

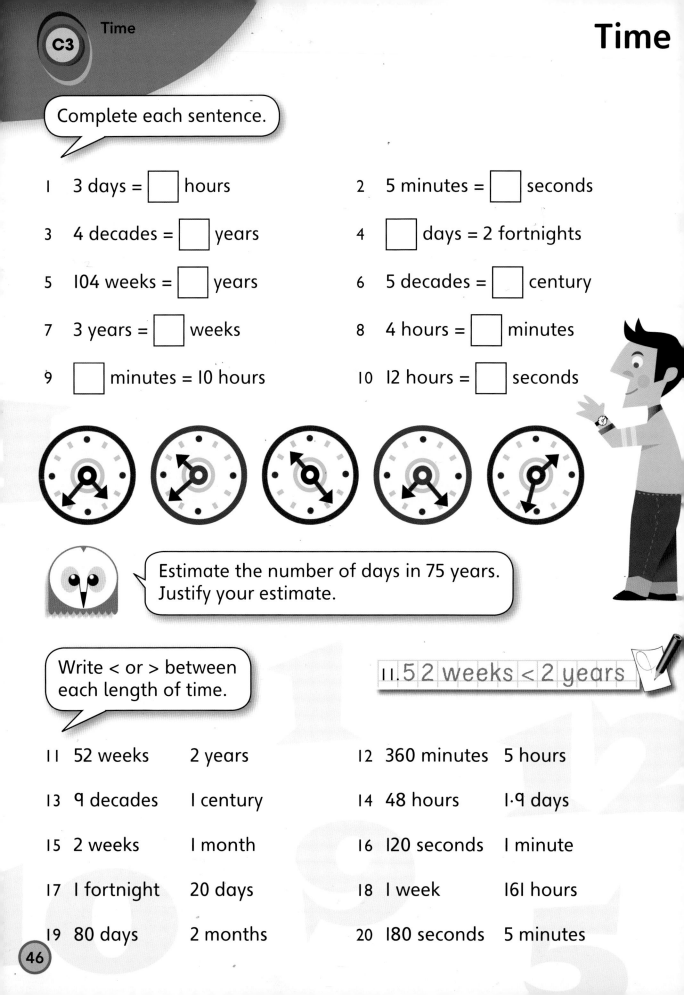

Estimate the number of days in 75 years. Justify your estimate.

Write < or > between each length of time.

11. 52 weeks < 2 years

11   52 weeks   2 years

12   360 minutes   5 hours

13   9 decades   1 century

14   48 hours   1·9 days

15   2 weeks   1 month

16   120 seconds   1 minute

17   1 fortnight   20 days

18   1 week   161 hours

19   80 days   2 months

20   180 seconds   5 minutes

Time

Write each unit of time in terms of two other units.

```
1. 1 hour
   6 0 minutes
    1   day
    2 4
```

1   hour

2   day

3   year

4   month

5   minute

6   decade

7   fortnight

8   century

Estimate how many leap years there are in a century. Work with a friend to find out.

True or false?

9
The number of days in February is equal to the number of years in three decades.

10
There are twice as many minutes in 5 hours as in 900 seconds.

11
There are more fortnights in a year than days in a month.

12
One year is 85 more days than 20 fortnights.

13
Fifty × 5 minutes is longer than $\frac{1}{6}$ day.

14
One week is more than 100 hours but less than 10 000 minutes.

Time

Write the number of days in each month.

1 July

2 September

3 April

4 January

5 December

6 May

7 October

8 March

9 February

10 June

11 November

12 August

We are told not to eat shellfish in months without an 'R' in their name. Discuss why this might be so.

Write the number of days between:

13. 28 days

13 3 October and 1 November

14 1 January and 14 February

15 25 December and 17 March

16 20 July and 4 September

17 1 May and 22 September

18 22 February and 22 September

19 4 July and 21 August

20 25 September and 24 November

21 18 February and 6 April

22 5 May and 30 August

23 3 July and 28 September

24 12 June and 15 October

Time

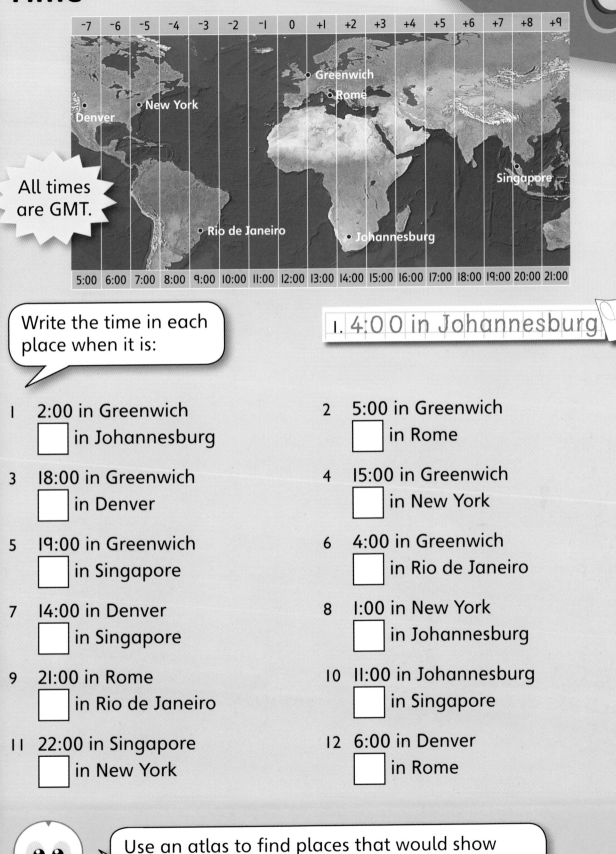

All times are GMT.

Write the time in each place when it is:

1. 4:00 in Johannesburg

1	2:00 in Greenwich	2	5:00 in Greenwich
	☐ in Johannesburg		☐ in Rome
3	18:00 in Greenwich	4	15:00 in Greenwich
	☐ in Denver		☐ in New York
5	19:00 in Greenwich	6	4:00 in Greenwich
	☐ in Singapore		☐ in Rio de Janeiro
7	14:00 in Denver	8	1:00 in New York
	☐ in Singapore		☐ in Johannesburg
9	21:00 in Rome	10	11:00 in Johannesburg
	☐ in Rio de Janeiro		☐ in Singapore
11	22:00 in Singapore	12	6:00 in Denver
	☐ in New York		☐ in Rome

Use an atlas to find places that would show the same time as each other on a 12-hour clock.

Reflections

Copy each shape. Draw the mirror.
Then draw the reflected shape.

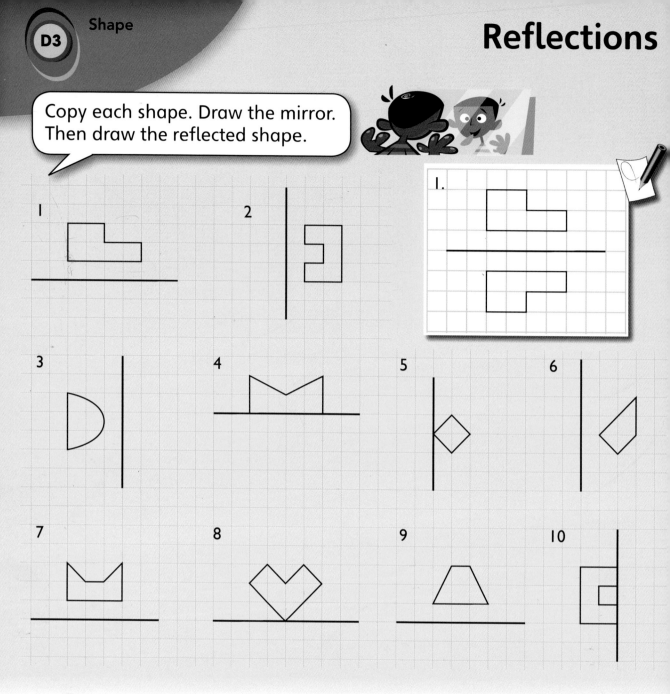

Use four different mirror positions to
reflect the first letter of your name.

Explore

Explore letters that are symmetrical when you reflect them in a
mirror line.

Reflections

Copy each shape. Draw the mirror.
Then draw the reflected shape.

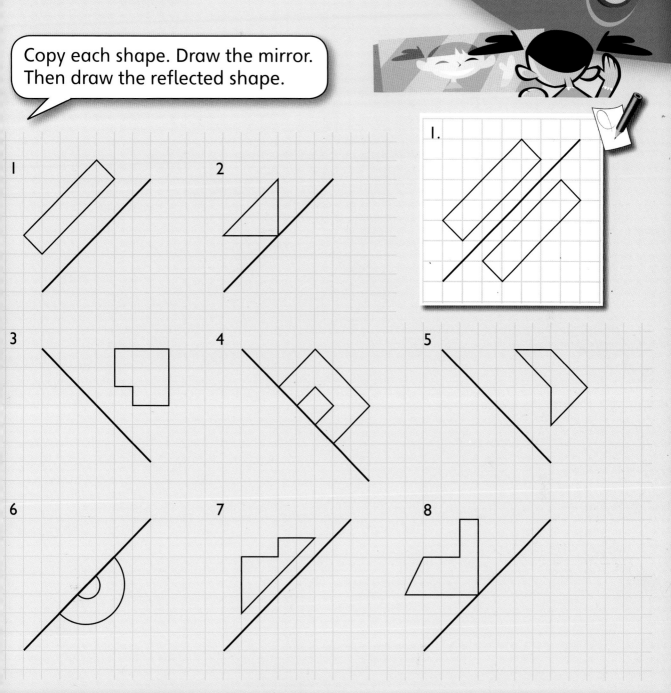

Explore

How many capital letters can be reflected in a vertical mirror and remain the right way round?

What about in a horizontal mirror?

51

Reflections

Draw each shape and the mirror lines.
Draw its reflection in both mirrors.

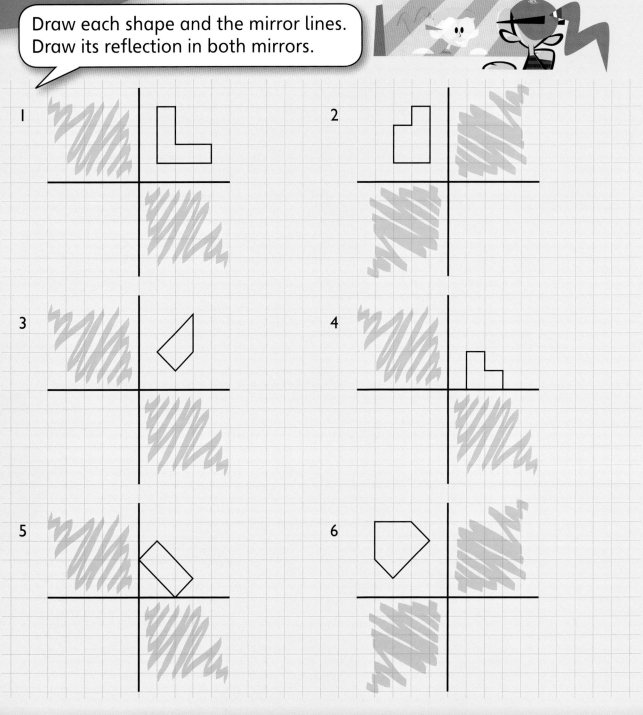

1

2

3

4

5

6

Explore

Reflect different quadrilaterals in two mirror lines. Try quadrilaterals with no lines of symmetry.

Reflections

Write the coordinates of each shape. Reflect the shape in both axes. Write the coordinates of the new shape.

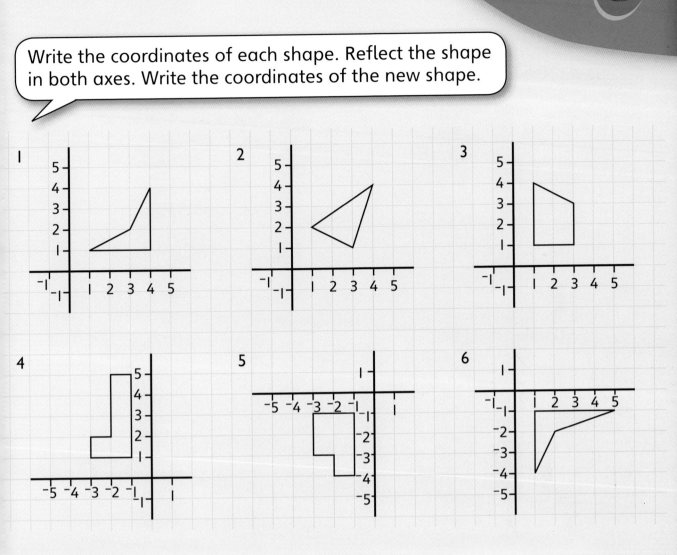

Draw two axes.
Draw a shape in the top left quadrant.
Write its coordinates.
Reflect it in both axes and write the new coordinates.

Write the coordinates that the shape will have if reflected in both axes.

7. (⁻2, ⁻2) (⁻2, ⁻1)...

7   (2, 2) (2, 1) (3, 1) (3, 2) (4, 4)

8   (3, 1) (4, 2) (1, 2)

9   (1, 1) (4, 1) (2, 3) (4, 3)

10   (2, 2) (3, 2) (1, 3) (1, 4) (3, 4)

53

Rotations

Draw the position after a rotation of 90° clockwise about the point.

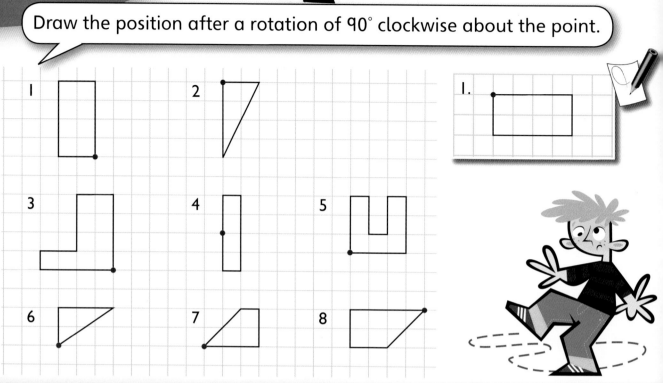

Find the matching shape after a rotation of 90° clockwise about the point.

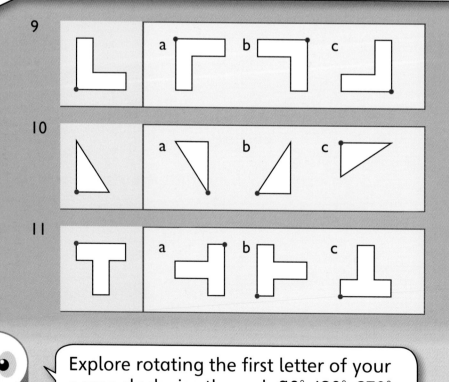

Explore rotating the first letter of your name clockwise through 90°, 180°, 270°.

Rotations

1

2

3

Rotate each shape about the point through:

a   180° clockwise

b   90° anticlockwise

c   270° clockwise

d   180° anticlockwise

e   90° clockwise

f   270° anticlockwise

Explore

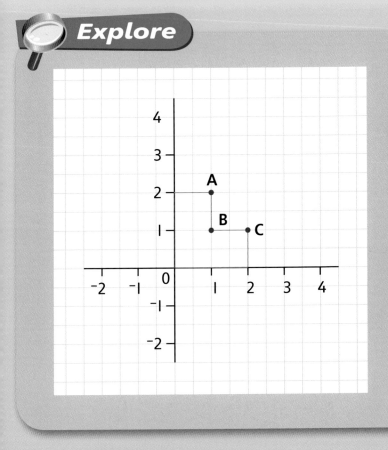

Rotate this shape 90° clockwise about point O. Write the new coordinates of points A, B, C.

Explore rotating about 180°, 270°.

Try other shapes.

Translations

Write the coordinates of each shape. Follow the instructions.
Write the new coordinates of the vertices.

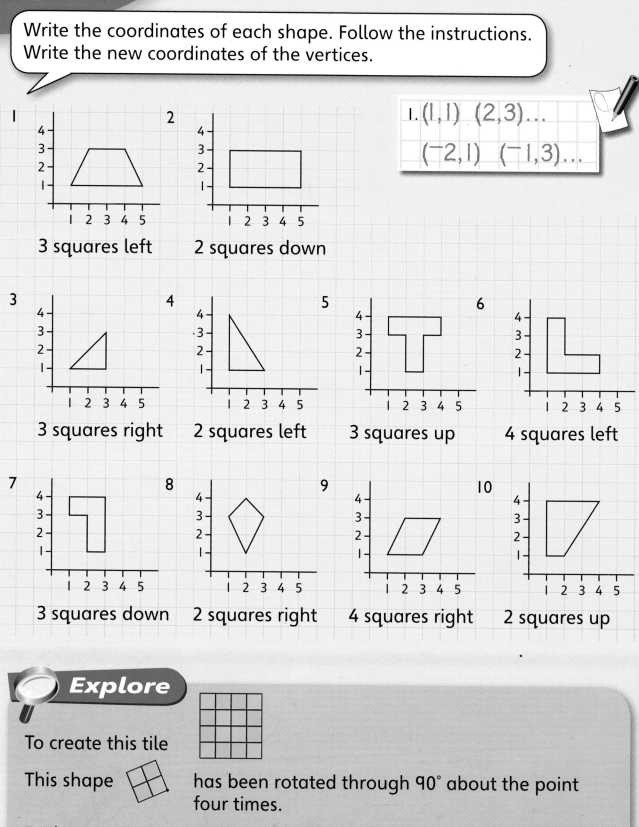

1. (1,1) (2,3)...
(‾2,1) (‾1,3)...

1

3 squares left

2

2 squares down

3

3 squares right

4

2 squares left

5

3 squares up

6

4 squares left

7

3 squares down

8

2 squares right

9

4 squares right

10

2 squares up

Explore

To create this tile

This shape has been rotated through 90° about the point four times.

Explore patterns rotating clockwise and anticlockwise. Try other tiles.

Translations

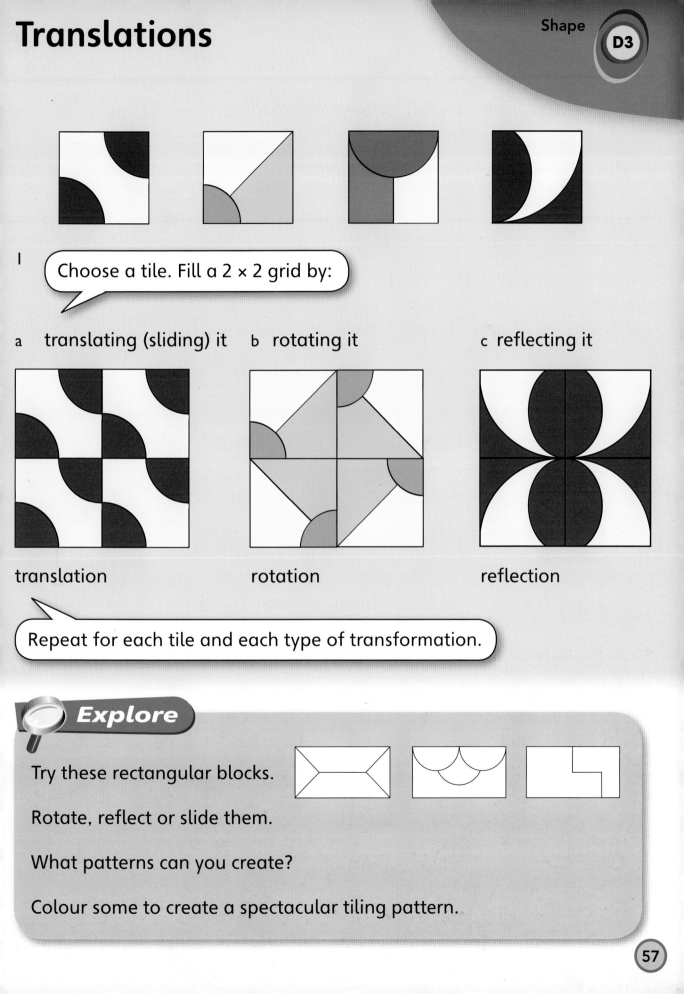

I

Choose a tile. Fill a 2 × 2 grid by:

a   translating (sliding) it
b   rotating it
c   reflecting it

translation

rotation

reflection

Repeat for each tile and each type of transformation.

🔍 Explore

Try these rectangular blocks.

Rotate, reflect or slide them.

What patterns can you create?

Colour some to create a spectacular tiling pattern.

Dividing

Copy and complete these divisions.

1.
```
  3)428
 − 300    100 × 3
   128
 − 120    40 × 3
     8
   ____     2 × 3
```

2.
```
  4)573
 − 400    100 × 4
   173
   ____    40 × 4
```

3.
```
  5)826
 − 500    100 × 5
   326
   ____
```

4. 4)464   5. 5)575   6. 3)369   7. 5)105

How many newspapers are there in each delivery?

8. 432 papers 3 deliveries

9. 517 papers 4 deliveries

10. 643 papers 5 deliveries

11. 974 papers 5 deliveries

12. 588 papers 3 deliveries

13. 724 papers 4 deliveries

14. 534 papers 3 deliveries

15. 821 papers 5 deliveries

16. 627 papers 4 deliveries

A newsagent has four paper girls and 636 papers to deliver. If one paper girl is ill, how many extra papers does each one deliver?

Dividing

Copy and complete.

1. $\begin{array}{r} \boxed{} \\ 3\overline{)416} \\ -300 \\ \hline \ldots \end{array}$

1 $3\overline{)416}$ 2 $5\overline{)627}$ 3 $4\overline{)739}$ 4 $726 \div 3$

5 $943 \div 4$ 6 $\dfrac{827}{3}$ 7 $623 \div 5$ 8 $4\overline{)862}$

Calculate the average number of visits to each website per day.

9

Mon	132
Tues	87
Weds	226
Thurs	148

10

Wed	346
Thurs	228
Fri	373

11

Sat	263
Sun	147
Mon	95
Tues	182
Wed	87

12

Sat	261
Sun	203
Mon	349
Tues	209

13

Tues	127
Wed	94
Thurs	109
Fri	156
Sat	172
Sun	213

14

Thurs	146
Fri	238
Sat	174

15

Mon	423
Tues	327
Wed	98

16

Fri	89
Sat	124
Sun	173
Mon	96
Tues	248

17

Mon	132
Tues	147
Wed	109
Thurs	94
Fri	135
Sat	126

Investigate how many visits each website could expect in the month of June.

Dividing

Complete each division.

1.
```
        20
        24
  18)432
    -360      20 × 18
       72
      -72      4 × 18
```

1 432 ÷ 18   2 434 ÷ 14

3 616 ÷ 22   4 864 ÷ 27

5 608 ÷ 32   6 748 ÷ 44   7 598 ÷ 23   8 646 ÷ 19

9 836 ÷ 38   10 378 ÷ 18   11 805 ÷ 35   12 384 ÷ 24

Calculate the average savings per month.

13 £432
18 months

14 £851
23 months

15 £806
31 months

16 £874
19 months

17 £553
14 months

18 £896
32 months

19 £901
17 months

20 £952
28 months

21 £736
16 months

Choose three divisions. Check your work by multiplying the answer by the divisor.

□□□ ÷ □□ = 23

Find numbers to fill the boxes to make this division work.

Dividing

Calculate the average amount raised by each child.

1.

```
        £4
       £4·23
30)1 2 6·9 0
  −1 2 0          £4 × 30
      6·9 0
     −6·0 0       20p × 30
        9 0
       −9 0       3p × 30
```

1 30 children
   raised £126·90

2 20 children
   raised £129·20

3 40 children
   raised £231·20

4 25 children
   raised £185·25

5 31 children
   raised £256·06

6 32 children
   raised £239·04

7 21 children
   raised £121·59

8 22 children
   raised £159·06

9 28 children
   raised £191·52

Choose three divisions. Check each by multiplying the answer by the divisor.

Explore

Some divisions can be made easier by halving both numbers, e.g.
1468 ÷ 18 = 734 ÷ 9

Or by halving, then halving again.
2364 ÷ 32 = 1182 ÷ 16 = 591 ÷ 8

Create some different divisions and show their easier versions.

Dividing decimals

Copy and complete.

1. ⑩
    4)53·2
    − 40   10 × 4
    ────
    13·2
    −12   3 × 4
    ────
    1·2
    −1·2   0·3 × 4
    ────

2. ⑳
    3)55·2
    − 30   10 × 3
    ────
    25·2
                8 × 3
    ────

3. ◯
    6)88·2
    − 60   10 × 6
    ────

    ────

4. 4)52·8

5. 3)36·9

6. 5)75·5

The runners in the relay race must run equal distances. Calculate how far each runs.

7. ⎡1 5⎤
    4)6 8·8

7. 4 runners 68·8 km

8. 3 runners 44·1 km

9. 4 runners 45·2 km

10. 3 runners 70·8 km

11. 4 runners 90·8 km

12. 3 runners 41·7 km

13. 6 runners 76·2 km

14. 3 runners 80·4 km

15. 4 runners 75·2 km

Choose one of the races. If it were 100 km long, how much further would each runner have to run?

Dividing decimals

Calculate the average weight of each vegetable.

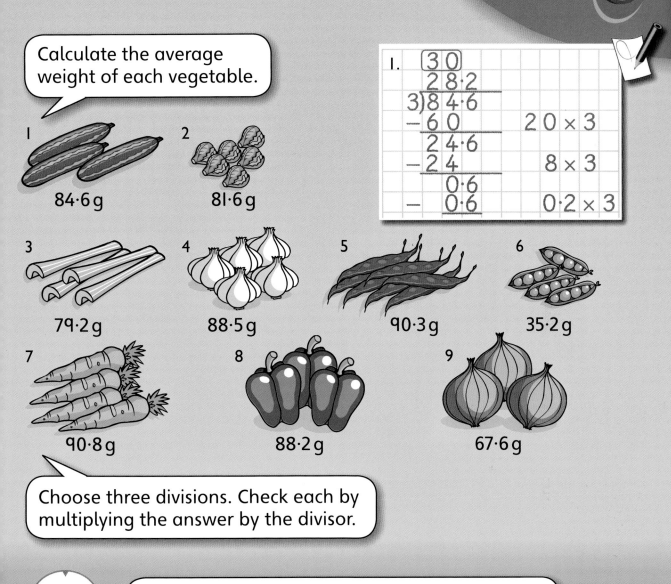

1.
```
      30
      28·2
 3)84·6
  -60        20 × 3
    24·6
   -24        8 × 3
     0·6
   -   0·6   0·2 × 3
```

1 84·6 g

2 81·6 g

3 79·2 g

4 88·5 g

5 90·3 g

6 35·2 g

7 90·8 g

8 88·2 g

9 67·6 g

Choose three divisions. Check each by multiplying the answer by the divisor.

With a partner, discuss approximately how many of each vegetable there are in 1 kilogram.

Complete these divisions.

10 4)58·8

11 3)70·8

12 6)73·2

13 8)94·4

14 6)98·4

15 3)96·9

16 4)86·4

17 6)82·2

18 4)95·6

63

Dividing decimals

These windows are regular polygons. Calculate the length of side of each window.

1.
```
        2
     1 · 8 2
  4)7 · 2 8
   - 4          1      × 4
     3 · 2 8
   - 3 · 2 0    0 · 8  × 4
     0 · 0 8
   - 0 · 0 8    0 · 0 2 × 4
```

1
P = 7·28 m

2
P = 8·76 m

3
P = 9·04 m

4
P = 8·22 m

5
P = 9·72 m

6
P = 6·95 m

Check each division by multiplying the answer by the divisor.

In this window, the perimeter is 8·42 m. Three sides are of equal length. Explore the possible lengths of the sides.

For each question, find the average length of fence painted per day.

7   82·02 m   3 days

8   73·84 m   4 days

9   68·2 m   5 days

10 89·74 m   1 week

11 96·42 m   3 days

12 70·68 m   6 days

13 84·92 m   4 days

14 87·08 m   1 week

15 79·38 m   3 days

Dividing decimals

Friends go out for a pizza, and split the bill equally. How much does each person pay?

1.
```
        8
        8. ...
  4) 3 3·3 6
    -3 2        8 × 4
        1·3 6
        ...
```

1 £33·36
4 people

2 £18·84
3 people

3 £44·76
6 people

4 £76·24
8 people

5 £47·04
7 people

6 £25·41
3 people

7 £51·36
4 people

8 £131·60
5 people

9 £166·14
9 people

To divide by a multiple of 10 you can use the trick of dividing both numbers by 10, e.g. 473·2 ÷ 30 = 47·32 ÷ 3. Use the trick to help with these divisions.

10 856·8 ÷ 40

11 883·8 ÷ 60

12 97·53 ÷ 30

13 886·9 ÷ 70

14 942·4 ÷ 80

15 975·6 ÷ 90

18·36 ÷ 0·3. Can you and your partner think of a trick to help you solve this division? What about 24·84 ÷ 0·04?

Proportion

Write the proportion of red marbles.
Write the fraction in its simplest form.

1. 4 out of 12
$$\frac{4}{12} = \frac{1}{3}$$

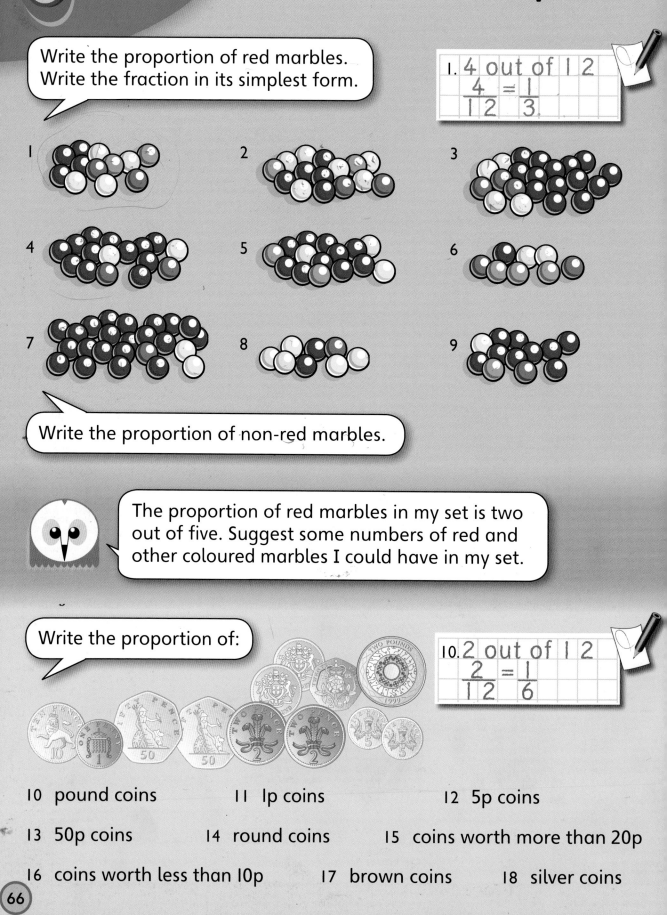

1

2

3

4

5

6

7

8

9

Write the proportion of non-red marbles.

The proportion of red marbles in my set is two out of five. Suggest some numbers of red and other coloured marbles I could have in my set.

Write the proportion of:

10. 2 out of 12
$$\frac{2}{12} = \frac{1}{6}$$

10 pound coins

11 1p coins

12 5p coins

13 50p coins

14 round coins

15 coins worth more than 20p

16 coins worth less than 10p

17 brown coins

18 silver coins

Proportion

Write the proportion of teams that have:

1. 5 out of 15
$$\frac{5}{15} = \frac{1}{3}$$

1   lost more than 5 matches

2   drawn more than 5 matches

3   played 20 matches

4   scored more than 50 points

5   won more than 10 matches

6   lost more than 10 matches

7   drawn more than 10 matches

8   scored between 30 and 50 points

9   played 22 matches

10   won 15 or more matches

11   lost fewer than 5 matches

12   scored fewer than 30 points

Abacus Premier League				
Played	Won	Drew	Lost	Points
Blackbird Rovers				
20	19	1	1	58
Wulverhampton Wanderers				
21	13	6	2	45
Carlton Athletic				
20	11	7	2	40
Dolton Wonderers				
21	14	1	6	43
Aston Miller				
22	9	6	7	33
Brotherwell				
20	16	2	2	50
Keen Spark Rangers				
21	7	6	8	27
Sheffield Thursday				
21	5	4	12	19
West Jam				
20	13	1	6	40
Oldcastle United				
21	9	8	4	35
Wagon Wanderers				
20	13	1	5	40
West Sandwich Albion				
22	8	1	3	25
Totem Pole Hotspurs				
21	12	6	3	42
Wimbleton				
20	17	2	3	53
Loverpool				
21	20	0	1	60

Which of the above proportions are greater than 50%? Look at the real premier league table. Write some proportion statements.

Proportion

The proportion of finches at the bird table is one out of four. How many finches can we expect to see if there are:

1 24 birds
2 32 birds

1. $\frac{1}{4}$ of 24 = 6 finches

3 16 birds
4 48 birds
5 120 birds?

If the proportion of robins is one out of eight, how many robins will you see in each case?

Three out of every eight cars that pass the Post Office are speeding! How many cars in total pass the Post Office if:

6. 3 out of 8
   6 out of 16
   16 cars go past

6 6 are speeding
7 9 cars are speeding

8 30 are speeding
9 15 are speeding

10 12 are speeding
11 24 are speeding

12 66 are speeding
13 25 cars are not speeding

14 55 cars are not speeding?

If the proportion of speeding cars drops to one out of four, how many cars must pass for the number of speeding cars to equal 25?

If the proportion of owls in a forest is one in ten of the night-time creatures, find possible animal population sizes.

Proportion

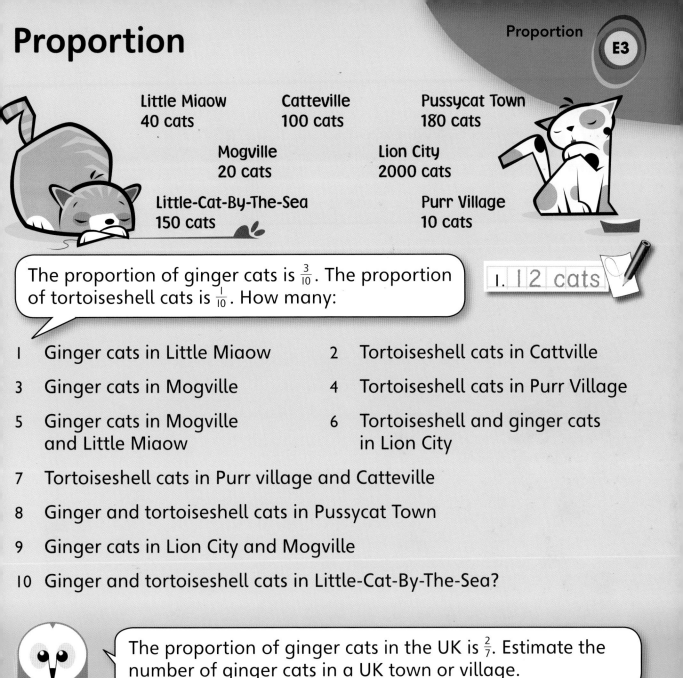

Little Miaow
40 cats

Catteville
100 cats

Pussycat Town
180 cats

Mogville
20 cats

Lion City
2000 cats

Little-Cat-By-The-Sea
150 cats

Purr Village
10 cats

The proportion of ginger cats is $\frac{3}{10}$. The proportion of tortoiseshell cats is $\frac{1}{10}$. How many:

1. 12 cats

1 Ginger cats in Little Miaow

2 Tortoiseshell cats in Cattville

3 Ginger cats in Mogville

4 Tortoiseshell cats in Purr Village

5 Ginger cats in Mogville and Little Miaow

6 Tortoiseshell and ginger cats in Lion City

7 Tortoiseshell cats in Purr village and Catteville

8 Ginger and tortoiseshell cats in Pussycat Town

9 Ginger cats in Lion City and Mogville

10 Ginger and tortoiseshell cats in Little-Cat-By-The-Sea?

The proportion of ginger cats in the UK is $\frac{2}{7}$. Estimate the number of ginger cats in a UK town or village.

11 Simon has 48 football stickers. One in four players wears a red shirt and two in six wears a blue shirt. How many players wearing red or blue shirts does he have?

12 One in twelve motorists owes car tax. Four out of five adults in Mathsland are motorists. If the adult population is 2400, how many owe car tax?

13 Three out of eight cat owners said their cat only eats tinned food and the same proportion said their cat only eats dried food. Out of 60 cat owners, how many have cats who don't eat tinned or dried food?

Ratio

Write the proportion of round beads in each necklace. Write the ratio of round to square.

1. $\frac{5}{8}$, 5:3

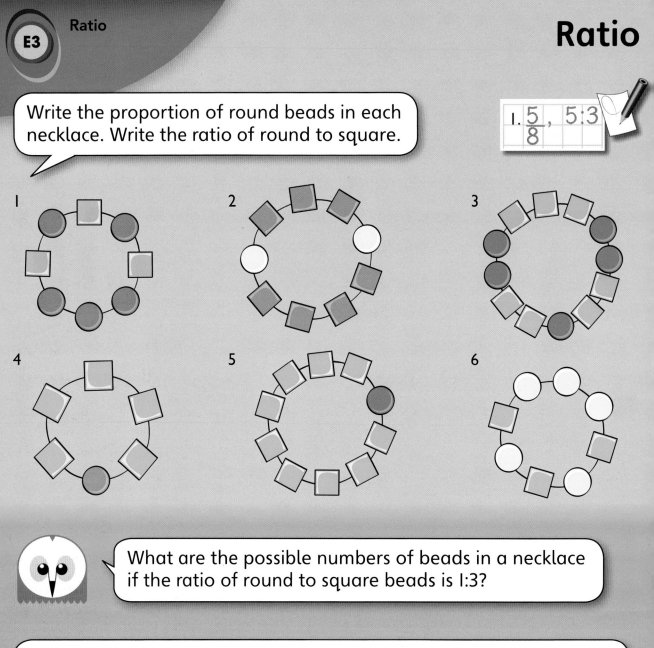

1   2   3

4   5   6

What are the possible numbers of beads in a necklace if the ratio of round to square beads is 1:3?

If the ratio of red to yellow tiles is 4:5, how many of each set are red?

7. 4 red

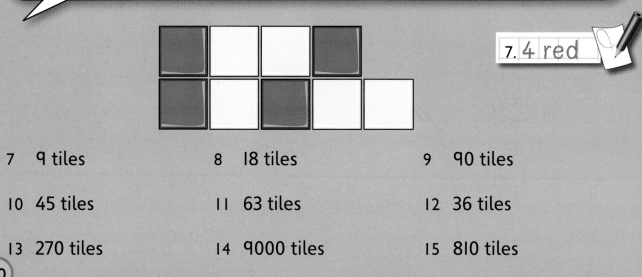

7 9 tiles	8 18 tiles	9 90 tiles
10 45 tiles	11 63 tiles	12 36 tiles
13 270 tiles	14 9000 tiles	15 810 tiles

Ratio

Write the proportion of patterned tiles.
Write the ratio of patterned tiles to plain.

1. $\dfrac{5}{10} = \dfrac{1}{2}$
$5:5 = 1:1$

1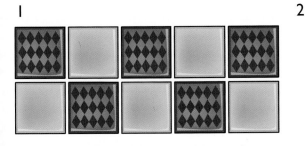

2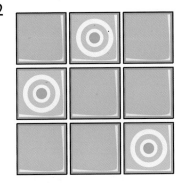

3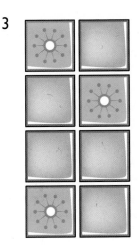

4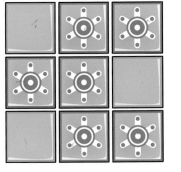

5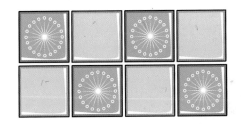

Investigate the ratio of either girls to boys in your class or children to adults in the school.

If the ratio of blue to orange tiles is 3:5, write the number of orange tiles in a set of:

6. $3 + 5 = 8$
10 tiles

6 16 tiles

7 40 tiles

8 800 tiles

9 24 tiles

10 56 tiles

11 320 tiles

Purple paint is created using two parts red paint to three parts blue paint. Write the number of tins of each paint needed to create:

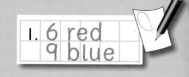

1. 6 red
   9 blue

| 1 | 15 tins | 2 | 30 tins | 3 | 50 tins |
| 4 | 5 tins | 5 | 100 tins | 6 | 60 tins |

Investigate the ratio of vowels to consonants in your name. What about your friends' names?

True or false?

7 Hair-dye is three parts gold to five parts brown. There are 150 ml of gold in 400 ml of dye.

8 Pink paint is five parts white to one part red. There is 1 litre of red in 1·2 l of paint.

9 Three out of eight marbles in a jar are red. There are 16 marbles that are not red in a jar of 24.

10 A ratio of 4:5 is the same as a proportion of $\frac{4}{9}$.

11 Four dogs out of every five dogs wear a collar. In a village of 100 dogs, there are 20 without collars.

12 The ratio of female to male cats in a street is 2:7. Out of 45 cats, ten are female.

Ratio

Sponge cake

Ratio of flour to sugar is 4:3

Ratio of sugar to fat is 3:1

2 eggs for every 100g of fat

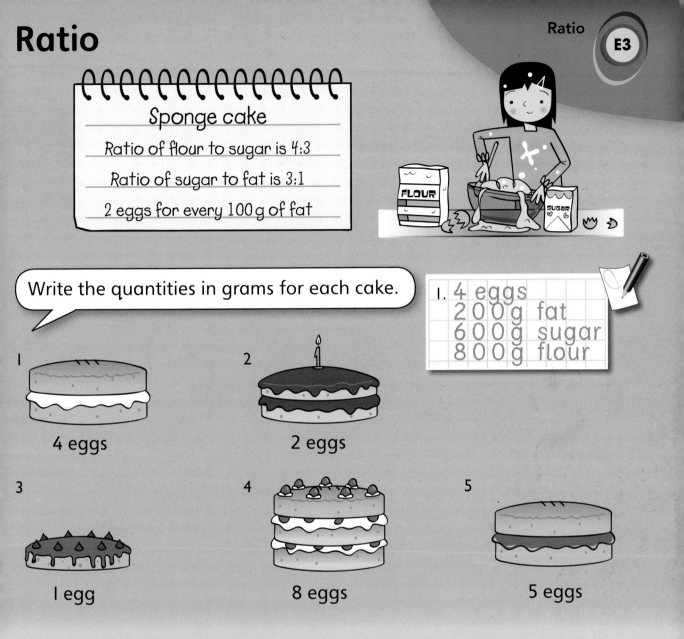

Write the quantities in grams for each cake.

1. 4 eggs
   200g fat
   600g sugar
   800g flour

1 4 eggs

2 2 eggs

3 1 egg

4 8 eggs

5 5 eggs

6 At a bird table, the ratio of robins to blue-tits is 1:4. If 24 blue tits visit regularly, how many robins visit?

7 In a mug of perfect tea, the ratio of tea to milk is 7:2. If a mug holds 270 ml, how much is milk? How much is tea?

8 If a swan's diet consists of worms and grain in a ratio of 3:5, how much grain in kg has she eaten if she has eaten 450g of worms?

In Benji's class, the ratio of children walking to those coming in a vehicle is 2:3. Investigate how many children there could be in the class and how many walked. How about your class?

Prime numbers

Copy this grid, or use the top of a 100-square. Loop all the prime numbers. Write how many there are.

1

1	2	3	4	5	6	7	8	9	10
11	12	13	14	15	16	17	18	19	20
21	22	23	24	25	26	27	28	29	30

Use a 100-square. Cross out number 1. Then cross out all the multiples of:

2   2, except 2 itself

3   3, except 3 itself

4   5, except 5 itself

5   7, except 7 itself

6   Highlight all the numbers left – the prime numbers. Check that you have 25 prime numbers altogether.

7   Is the number of prime numbers less than 50 the same as for between 50 and 100?

8   Write how many prime numbers there are between:

a   1 and 20   b   20 and 40   c   40 and 60   d   60 and 80

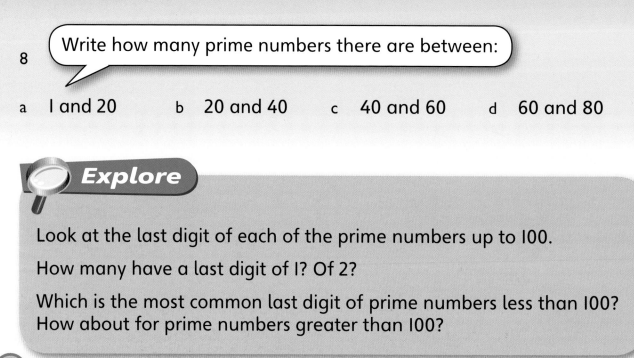

Explore

Look at the last digit of each of the prime numbers up to 100.

How many have a last digit of 1? Of 2?

Which is the most common last digit of prime numbers less than 100? How about for prime numbers greater than 100?

Prime numbers

Are these prime numbers? Write 'yes' or 'no'.

1	23	2	5	3	19	4	27	5	15	6	29

7	31	8	21	9	39	10	99	11	33	12	75

For each 'no' answer, investigate which is the nearest prime number.

Write all the prime numbers in each set.

13   6   4   7   3   5   11   9   12

14   13   14   12   22   18   19   15   17

15   29   33   31   35   27   41   62   25

16   43   63   45   49   52   47   51   44   58   55

Write the next prime number after:

17	12	18	9	19	3	20	15	21	22	22	26	23	30	24	34

25	42	26	50	27	60	28	25	29	35	30	70	31	80	32	45

Explore

17 and 71 are 'reverse' numbers, and they are both prime numbers.
Investigate how many more pairs like this you can find.

Prime numbers

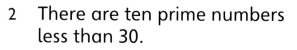

True or false?

1   All prime numbers are odd numbers.

2   There are ten prime numbers less than 30.

3   All prime numbers have exactly two factors.

4   The total of two prime numbers is always an even number.

5   Every number next to a multiple of 6 is a prime number.

6   Every 2-digit prime number is next to a multiple of 6.

7   Every 2-digit multiple of 6 is next to a prime number.

8   There is only one 2-digit prime number that has 6 as a tens digit.

9   I is not a prime number.

10 All 2-digit prime numbers have a units digit of I, 3, 7 or 9.

11 There are four prime numbers between 10 and 20.

12 A square number cannot be a prime number.

Explore

Large primes are used as security codes because they are difficult to crack.

Find some prime numbers greater than 100. Try to find some very large ones. Use the test for divisibility to help you.

Did you know? The largest prime number has over 20 digits!

Explore

These pairs of prime numbers have a total of 90.   7 and 83

Can you find seven more pairs like this?   II and 79

Prime numbers

I am a prime number. Who am I?

1   I am between 20 and 70. My digits total 10.

2   I am the fourth prime number after 40.

3   I am a 2-digit number. My digits have a difference of 7.

4   I am between 25 and 42. My units digit is a prime number.

5   I am the third prime number after 20.

6   I am between 40 and 80. When my digits are reversed I am another prime number.

Explore

Use cards 1–9 to make prime numbers.

four prime numbers using six cards: 31   47   2   5

four prime numbers using seven cards: 61   29   47   3

Investigate different ways. Can you use more than seven cards?

Explore

On squared paper, copy and continue this number spiral up to 80.

Colour the prime numbers.

Describe any patterns they make.

	3	4	5
11	2	1	6
10	9	8	7

Prime factors

Copy and complete these divisions to find the prime factors.

1

2	40
2	20
2	
5	

2

2	12
	6

3

2	16
2	

4

2	30
3	

5

	24

6

	20

7

	52

8

	35

Write the list of prime factors for each number.

1. prime factors of 40: $2 \times 2 \times 2 \times 5$

Find three numbers that each have three prime factors.

Find the prime factors of:

9 8   10 14   11 18   12 27   13 28   14 26   15 32   16 45

17 Copy and complete this table:

Number	Prime factors
20	2 × 2 × 5
21	3 × 7
22	2 × 11
...	
40	

Prime factors

Copy and complete these factor trees.

1.
```
        36
       /  \
      2    18
          /  \
         2    9
             / \
```

2.
```
        50
       /  \
      2    25
          /  \
```

3.
```
        28
       /  \
      2    14
          /  \
```

4.
```
        48
       /  \
      2   [ ]
          / \
```

5.
```
        56
       /  \
     [ ]   28
          / \
```

6.
```
        60
       /  \
     [ ]  [ ]
     / \
```

Write the list of prime factors for each number.

1. 36 = 2 × 2 × 3 × 3

Explore

All the numbers in questions 1–6 have 2 as a prime factor. Can you find some that don't? Write a list of those that have only 2 as a prime factor, e.g. 8.

Find the prime factors of:

7 38	8 18	9 51	10 54
11 57	12 42	13 104	14 70
15 144	16 120	17 108	18 250

Prime factors

🔍 Explore

Investigate all the numbers that have exactly two 1-digit prime factors.

How many different numbers are there?

Investigate numbers that have exactly one 1-digit and one 2-digit prime factors, e.g. $39 = 3 \times 13$.

> Draw a multiplication table for the 1-digit prime numbers.

> Multiply to find the numbers that have these as their prime factors.

1. $2 \times 2 \times 3 = 12$

1 $2 \times 2 \times 3$	2 $2 \times 3 \times 5$
3 $2 \times 3 \times 3 \times 3$	4 $3 \times 5 \times 7$
5 $2 \times 3 \times 11$	6 $3 \times 3 \times 7$
7 $2 \times 3 \times 5 \times 7$	8 $2 \times 2 \times 2 \times 2 \times 2$
9 $3 \times 3 \times 3$	10 $5 \times 5 \times 5$
11 $3 \times 7 \times 11$	12 $2 \times 5 \times 17$

🔍 Explore

Investigate numbers up to 60 that have more than two prime factors.

$20 = 2 \times 2 \times 5$ three prime factors

$36 = 2 \times 2 \times 3 \times 3$ four prime factors